Growing Up in Multi-Faith Britain

Religion, Education and Culture

Series Editors:
William K. Kay (University of Wales, Bangor, UK),
Leslie J. Francis (University of Wales, Bangor, UK) and
Jeff Astley (University of Durham, UK)

This series addresses issues raised by religion and education within contemporary culture. It is intended to be of benefit to those involved in professional training as ministers of religion, teachers, counsellors, psychologists, social workers and health professionals while also contributing to the theoretical development of the academic fields from which this training is drawn.

Growing Up in Multi-Faith Britain

Explorations in youth, ethnicity and religion

by

A. G. C. SMITH

on behalf of The International Seminar on
Religious Education and Values (ISREV)

UNIVERSITY OF WALES PRESS
CARDIFF
2007

© A. G. C. Smith, 2007

All rights reserved. No part of this book may be reproduced, stored in a retrieval system, or transmitted, in any form or by any means, electronic, mechanical, photocopying, recording or otherwise, without clearance from the University of Wales Press, 10 Columbus Walk, Brigantine Place, Cardiff, CF10 4UP. www.wales.ac.uk/press

British Library Cataloguing-in-Publication Data
A catalogue record for this book is available from the British Library.

ISBN Paperback: 978-0-7083-2071-6
ISBN Hardback: 978-0-7083-2056-3

The rights of A. G. C. Smith to be identified as author of this work has been asserted by him in accordance with sections 77 and 79 of the Copyright, Designs and Patents Act 1988.

Typeset by Florence Production Ltd, Stoodleigh, Devon
Printed in Great Britain by Antony Rowe Ltd, Wiltshire

Contents

Acknowledgements	vii
Introduction	1
1. Britain: a nation in transition	4
2. The religious affiliation and practices of teenagers in Britain	18
3. Well-being and mental health	23
4. Relating to other people	31
5. Sexual morality	41
6. Questions of right and wrong	54
7. Substance use and abuse	62
8. Free time and leisure pursuits	70
9. Education and schools	78
10. Work and employment	85
11. Global and national concerns	95
12. Young people and politics	102
13. Religious beliefs in the contemporary world	111
14. Conclusions and recommendations	119
Appendices	131
Notes	137
Bibliography	149
Glossary and abbreviations	166
Index	168

Acknowledgements

Many people have offered help and advice as I have written this book and I would like to thank them: Professor Leslie Francis of the University of Wales (Bangor) who supervised the research upon which this book is based; Helen Glover and Mandy Robbins for help with the questionnaires; and Hilary Fairfield who read the draft text and made a number of helpful observations.

Introduction

The origins of this book lie in a sabbatical in 1996 when I studied the religious practices and beliefs of teenagers in Walsall in the West Midlands of the United Kingdom. I was interested in how religious practices and beliefs might influence attitudes and behaviour.

For some years I had been aware of the Teenage Religion and Values Initiative,[1] a project studying British adolescents, which has been running for about thirty years (Francis, 1982, 1984; Francis and Kay, 1995). It has explored the relationship between beliefs, behaviour and attitudes (Kay and Francis, 1996: 1–9) and has shown that religion and personality type are important factors in understanding a wide range of issues from drug use to environmental pollution (Francis, 1996 and 1997).[2] This project has accumulated a substantial body of data examining young people's attitudes to personal and public morality, and to a range of institutions such as the church, government and the education system.

Kay and Francis have expressed the hope 'that scholars working in other religious traditions will wish to extend our quest by both replicating some of our earlier studies and developing new studies with comparable instruments designed to measure attitude towards other religions' (Kay and Francis, 1996: 9). My research was an attempt to do that[3] and this book seeks to place the fruit of that research in the public domain and to make its findings available to academics, community leaders and policy-makers. The focus of this book, however, is much wider than the beliefs and attitudes of teenagers in the West Midlands. The terrorist attacks in the United States of America on 11 September 2001 provoked a widespread interest in the influence of religion (and particularly Islam) on young people and have generated a mass of new research, articles and books. In writing this book I have taken the opportunity to draw upon material from a wide range of sources and research, in order to reflect on the experiences of young British people as they grow up in a multi-faith and multicultural society. I hope that in making available both the raw data and my analysis of it this study will contribute towards a deeper understanding of the influence of religion on young people today.

The contents of the book

In the opening chapter of the book I describe the context in which my research is set and is to be evaluated, by painting a broad-brush canvas of the effect of the decline in social capital and concerns about race and immigration. I also comment on the importance of religion in the light of the terrorist attacks in the United States of America. In the second chapter I examine the role of religion in the lives of teenagers in Britain today and their attitudes to their own religious tradition.

In chapter 3 I turn to the first of eleven specific areas of concern to teenagers and how religion may have a bearing on them. It focuses on the sense of well-being and mental health of young people. Do they find life is worth living and do they have a sense of purpose? Chapter 4 explores the responses of the teenagers when they were asked whether they wanted someone to talk with about their problems, and, if so, whether they preferred to speak to professionals, to family members or to friends. Chapter 5 reflects on a number of areas such as extramarital sex, divorce, contraception, abortion and gay issues. A range of issues are explored in chapter 6 under the general heading of 'Right and Wrong', such as stealing, lying, graffiti, truancy, shoplifting, alcohol and smoking.

In chapter 7 I analyse their attitudes towards substance use and abuse and in particular the use of alcohol, tobacco and other drugs. Chapter 8 is an examination of the young people's attitudes towards leisure and parental attitudes towards the way in which the teenagers use their time. Chapter 9 looks at the adolescents' views of their education and more specifically their opinions of their school, exams, their fellow pupils and teachers. It also looks at the worries that some pupils experience in relation to exams and bullying.

Chapter 10 examines attitudes towards employment and job satisfaction and chapter 11 explores 'Global and National Concerns' by focusing on those wider issues that may concern teenagers, such as the threat of nuclear war, Third World poverty, environmental pollution, portrayals of violence in the media, pornography and the National Lottery.

Local and national politics are examined in chapter 12, when the young people are asked about party politics, education, trades unions and immigration. In chapter 13 I turn specifically to religion and the beliefs of the teenagers as they grow up in their different faith communities.

In the concluding chapter I draw these various strands together in order to reflect on the cumulative influence that different religions and faith communities are having on young people in Britain today. As a consequence I suggest a number of ways in which the findings of this research has serious implications for policy-makers at both national and local levels, whether they be politicians, educationalists, employers or health-care professionals.

1
Britain: a nation in transition

1.1 Introduction

The world is becoming an increasingly complex place to live in. Over recent decades the rate of change has accelerated. In traditional societies the older generation acts as the repository of knowledge and wisdom, and the elderly are given a place of honour by the younger generation. Rapid changes in Western society, such as greatly increased personal wealth, a wide range of new technologies and a breakdown in traditional patterns of family life, have turned this upside down. Today in the West it is the younger generation who set the pace. Compared with previous generations they have been given unparalleled freedom and choice. One consequence of this change is a widespread angst about society in general and the younger generation in particular, which has resulted in more writing about young people in Britain today than in any previous generation. There are numerous articles, television programmes and books about youth cultures which try to understand the complexities of the postmodern world of today's young people. An example of this is a book by Rutter and Smith which highlighted a number of key findings:

> Recorded crime (mostly committed by young people) increased tenfold in Britain between 1950 and 1993; nearly all developed countries have seen substantial increases in psychosocial disorders among youth since the Second World War; use of illicit drugs and drug dependency was low for those born in 1940, but rose rapidly after 1950; suicide rates in Europe have increased throughout the twentieth century, with the most striking rise among young males between 1970 and 1990.
> (Reported in *The Times*, 30 May 1995)

History shows that every generation worries about its young people and is concerned about an apparent decline in standards and values. One radio broadcaster has even coined the phrase 'generational envy' to describe the phenomenon of older people looking jealously at the young. All this may be true, but what is equally clear is that we are currently experiencing change at an unprecedented rate and of a totally different kind than has been seen before. The speed of change at the end of the twentieth and the beginning of the twenty-first centuries has probably widened the gap between adults and teenagers more than in any previous generation, with the result that, although many adults think they know what young people are worried about, research reveals that the young people themselves often view things quite differently.[1]

Underlying this pervasive anxiety about young people are a number of major shifts in the way in which society is structured and how it functions. The decline in social capital in Britain, concerns about race, asylum seekers, the growing influence of Islam (especially since the terrorist attacks of 11 September 2001 in the United States of America and other bombings in Bali, Madrid and most recently in London) and more generally about the role of religion are all causes of concern and to these we now turn.

1.2 Individualism and the decline in social capital

Social capital is about the levels of trust and mutual support in communities.[2] In particular it refers to the way people contribute to the good of society by caring and taking responsibility for others, by social and charitable work, and the extent to which they trust one another. It is widely assumed that individualism appears to be increasing and there is a perception that people are less willing to be involved in their local community than in the past. In other words, social capital is declining. Wilkinson and Mulgan have charted the decline in membership of those belonging to, for example, political parties, the National Federation of Women's Institutes, the Mother's Union and the National Union of Townswomen's Guilds (1995: 101). The decline in attendance in organized religion (Currie, Gilbert and Horsley, 1977; Gill, 1993 and 2003), membership of trades unions (Bryson and Gomez, 2002: 44–5), and in giving to charities (Leach, 1999)[3] are all well documented. However, research reveals that the changes are even starker among the young. Thus it has been demonstrated that, compared with a few years earlier, young people are far less likely to vote in local, national or European elections (Park, 2004: 38–9), a smaller proportion of them think voting is a civil duty (Park, 1999: 37) and they are less likely to be attached to a political party than older people (Park, 2000: 9). The government has become so worried about this trend that it introduced postal voting in the 2004 elections in an attempt to increase the number of people who vote. There is some concern that young people are less willing to undertake voluntary or charitable work than in the past.

There is also some evidence of changes in attitudes among young people towards themselves and society in general. For example, Halpern's study of young people across Europe concluded that

> there has been a reduction in the universality of norms, values and constraints at the informal level. This was manifested by higher levels of individualism (emphasis on individual convictions rather than external models), the development of libertarian (as opposed to authoritarian) values, and higher levels of tolerance in the personal sphere in general.
> (1995: 383)

Some commentators argue that these changes represent a fundamental shift in British society. For example, Wilkinson and Mulgan (1995) refer to 'a deep seated rejection of society's central institutions' (p. 105), 'an historic political disconnection' (p. 99), and a 'potentially explosive alienation' (p. 113) among young people. This rejection of the traditional political system is illustrated by a growing willingness of younger people to take to the street in direct action (Wilkinson and Mulgan, 1995: 104) and the increasing sense of alienation among many young people who feel disconnected from the democratic system (Wilkinson and Mulgan, 1995: 106). The same phenomenon was seen in protests during the building of new roads at Twyford Down and Bathampton during the 1990s and most recently over the Iraq war.

The causes of these changes are harder to identify. Some point to the Thatcherism of the 1980s ('There is no such thing as society'), to increased personal wealth after a long period of peace, to the stress on individual rights (as exemplified by the European Convention of Human Rights, which came into force in Britain on 2 October 2000) and by the government's introduction of, for example, Patients' Charters in the National Health Service. The emphasis has been consistently on individual rights rather than civic duties. Such is the level of concern about the decline in social capital that *The Sunday Times* (27 July 2003), under a headline 'Palace bid to rebuild a trusting nation' reported that 'a number of eminent sociologists [were] summoned to the palace to discuss the problem with a group of the Queen's senior advisers'. The meeting had been prompted by a report compiled by David Halpern that showed that 'the level of trust between strangers in Britain had halved in the past 40 years'.

Much research has been undertaken in order to understand the nature of social capital, how it is changing and the factors that influence it. It has been established that there is a clear correlation between involvement in organizations and social trust. For example, in their research on social capital Johnston and Jowell compare membership of organizations (such as community, countryside, sports, cultural, religion and church attendance) with the proportion of people who think that 'most people can be trusted'. The results are striking. For example, only 42 per cent of those who do not belong to a community organization agree that 'most people can be trusted', compared with 57 per cent of those who belong to two or more community organizations. There is also a marked difference between those who do not belong to a religion, or rarely attend worship, with those who are regular attendees. For example, only 45 per cent of those who do not belong to a religion agree that 'most people can be trusted', compared with 50 per cent of those belong to a religion and attend church once a week or more frequently (Johnston and Jowell, 2001: 183). The relationship between, for example, churchgoing and social capital has been well documented (Smith, 2005).

1.3 Multiculturalism and cultural identity

Alongside concerns about a decline in social capital, there has been a debate about multiculturalism and 'Britishness'. The background to this can be traced to five main areas: large-scale immigration into Britain over the past fifty years; racial unrest and violence in the inner cities, the extent to which the South Asian British[4] communities are integrating; the growth in Islam and terrorist attacks (such as 11 September 2001); and the clash of Western and Asian cultures. Each of these areas merits closer scrutiny in order to understand the context in which this study is set.

1.3.1 Large-scale immigration

For many centuries Britain has welcomed immigrants (Berthoud and Beishon, 1997: 18–59; Visram, 2002: 1–360), although the numbers were relatively small. Following the Second World War there was a large influx of people, initially from the West Indies, and then from the Indian subcontinent. At the 2001 census 13 per cent of the population of England and 4 per cent of the population of Wales gave their ethnic origin as other than White British. The overall figures for the United Kingdom showed that ethnic minorities made up 8 per cent of the population. Never before in the history of Britain has there been such a large influx of people in so short a space of time. Looking to the future, the proportion of the UK population from ethnic minority backgrounds is set to increase, due to continued immigration, larger families and a lower average age.[5]

The scale of current immigration has not been without its critics, most notably Enoch Powell MP, whose opposition reached its height in his speech on 13 April 1968 in the West Midlands. In the last few years the higher profile of the British National Party in local and European elections has raised deep concerns. Most recently Trevor Phillips, the chairman of the Commission for Racial Equality, called for the abandonment of multiculturalism, which he claimed was no longer useful since it is encouraging separateness (*Observer*, 4 April 2004). Such are the sensitivities over immigration that the immigration minister, Beverley Hughes, resigned at the end of March 2004 over claims that the Home Office had allowed thousands of 'fraudulent' immigrants into the United Kingdom from Romania. There have been worries about the rise in the number of asylum seekers. In 2002 the debate came to a head, focusing on the Red Cross Refugee Centre at Sangatte near Calais and a spate of stories about illegal asylum seekers being found on lorries and on the trains coming through the Channel Tunnel.

On 1 May 2004 an additional ten countries became members of the European Union. There were worries that Britain would be swamped with workers from eastern Europe, attracted by higher wages and better living conditions. In the event, this has not happened, but it did not stop Britain's membership of the European Union becoming a major theme in the European Elections that occurred shortly after. The United Kingdom Independence Party campaigned on a platform of withdrawal from the European Union, although it did not make much headway. In December 2004 there was a debate about the decision of the European Union to begin the process to allow Turkey, a predominantly Muslim country, to join.

Issues of immigration and asylum have been closely monitored by Migration Watch UK, which has been campaigning against the relatively open policy of the British government. Despite this, the number of immigrants has increased dramatically since 1998, possibly due to the introduction into British law of the European Convention of Human Rights and Fundamental Freedoms (McLaren and Johnson, 2004: 170–1). During the same period there has been an increase in the proportion of people who are unhappy about the level of immigration and would like to see it changed (McLaren and Johnson, 2004: 172–3). In response to the concerns about immigration and asylum in 2004, the government has introduced stricter criteria for British citizenship, which includes a knowledge of British history, basic tests in the English language and lessons about life in Britain, as well as a citizenship ceremony.

1.3.2 Racial unrest and violence in inner cities

Most of the immigrants have settled in a relatively small number of urban areas[6] and consequently many White British people do not encounter black and Asian people on a regular basis. Much of their knowledge of immigrants comes primarily from the media. Most of the time white, black and Asian communities have lived together peacefully. Nevertheless, there have been a number of disturbances involving conflict between young black, Asian and white men. As early as 1958 there were race riots in Dudley, Nottingham and Notting Hill. In 1981 there was unrest and violence on the streets of Brixton, Toxteth and the St Paul's district of Bristol, which resulted in an inquiry and subsequent report by Lord Scarman. In 1985 there were disturbances in the Handsworth area of Birmingham. Trouble also flared up in the summer of 2001 in Bradford, Oldham, Burnley and Stoke-on-Trent and in Lozells in Birmingham in October 2005, when a man was stabbed to death.[7]

1.3.3 South Asian British communities: integration or separation?

Immigrants to Britain came with their ethnic customs and religious beliefs. Initially many of them presumed that they would stay for only a few years and return home. Gradually this expectation began to change and within a few years they were building mandirs, mosques and gurdwaras. For most of the time there have been few problems with their living in British society. Periodically an issue has arisen which has hit the headlines, such as whether Sikh bus conductors should be allowed to wear their turbans or whether they had to wear crash helmets when riding motorcycles. More recently there have been disagreements over whether Muslim girls had to wear school uniforms. For example, in June 2004 a fifteen-year-old Muslim, Shabina Begum, lost her case in the High Court in which she hoped to overturn her school's decision not to allow her to wear the jilbab. This was followed by a ban on girls' wearing strict Islamic dress to school in Tower Hamlets, resulting in some girls being withdrawn from school (*The Times*, 7 November 2004).[8] In March 2005 Shabina Begum won her case on appeal (*Guardian*, 3 March 2005).

Religious and ethnic practices are still at the heart of South Asian communities in Britain, but the situation is not open to simple analysis. On the one hand, many of the older members of the community worry that their young people are losing touch with their roots. For example, an article in *The Times* (3 September 1999) examined the extent to which traditional Asian communities are breaking down and argued that young people have become more Westernized, more assertive and more likely to drink alcohol and take drugs. Although it was suggested that young people from South Asian communities would still listen to the older generation, they were less willing to put up with many of the things that their parents had simply accepted. On the other hand, another group of young South Asian Britons have rediscovered their cultural and religious roots, and have adopted traditional styles of dress and customs. Thus, a significant number of young Sikh men have chosen to wear the turban again and many young Muslim girls have adopted the hijab. Some of these young people are more zealous and committed in their religious beliefs and observances than their parents' generation.[9]

1.3.4 The growth in Islam, Islamophobia and 11 September 2001

As well as a significant growth in the number of Muslims in Britain over the past fifty years, there have been a number of events that have raised the profile of the Muslim community, such as the Salman Rushdie affair. In September 1988 his book *The Satanic Verses* was published. It was condemned by a number of international Muslim bodies. Paradoxically its publication acted as a rallying point for a wide range of disparate Muslim groups who had never cooperated before. Demonstrations took place in Birmingham and in Bradford. In January 1989 a group of Muslims burned the book publicly in Bradford and on 14 February Ayatollah Khomeini pronounced a fatwa on Rushdie. There was an immediate response from a wide range of Westerners against the Muslims' call for censorship and the fatwa. One of the striking things about the episode was the almost total lack of comprehension by many Westerners about why many Muslims found the book so offensive and it revealed a lack of awareness about the South Asian British communities and their religious beliefs.

Since the terrorist attack on the World Trade Centre in New York on 11 September 2004 attention has turned again to the influence of religion and in particular of Islam. Subsequent terrorist acts (such as the bombings in Bali in October 2002 and in October 2005 and the attack on the commuter trains in Madrid in March 2004) have raised the profile of radical Muslims even higher. In the United Kingdom there has been a deep sense of puzzlement about why a number of young Muslim men, born and brought up in Britain, many of whom have received a Western education, should travel to Afghanistan or Iraq and sign up to fight with the terrorist movement Al Qaida.[10] The subsequent detention by the Americans of a number of South Asian British men in the camp at Guantanamo Bay only served to complicate matters further. The London bombings on 7 July 2005 and the attempted bombings on 21 July (with headlines such as those in the *Daily Telegraph* of 23 July 2005: 'One in four Muslims sympathises with motives of terrorists') has kept the matter high on the political agenda in the United Kingdom.

One of the Islamic groups in the UK which has caused particular unease is al-Muhajiroun, a radical group which is led by a Syrian-born preacher Sheikh Omar Bakri Mohammed and which claims to have about two thousand followers in Britain. It was one of his followers from Britain, Asif Mohammed Hanif, who carried out the suicide bombing in Tel Aviv at the end of April 2003 which killed three Israelis. In April 2004 an undercover newspaper reporter recorded speakers at an al-Muhajiroun meeting saying that Lord Ahmed, a Labour peer, should be killed for committing 'apostasy' (*The Sunday Times*, 18 April 2004). On 4 April 2004 the *Observer* reported that members of al-Muhajiroun had burned the Union Jack outside the Central Mosque in Regent's Park, London.

These deep anxieties have provoked a vigorous debate. For example, the former Archbishop of Canterbury, Dr George Carey criticized the Muslim leadership in Britain in a lecture at the Gregorian University in Rome in March 2004, saying 'We look to them [moderate Muslims] to condemn suicide bombers and terrorists who use Islam as a weapon to destabilise and destroy innocent lives . . .' (Carey, 2004: 9). In the same month the Muslim Council of Britain wrote to more than one thousand mosques, asking them to exercise vigilance against terrorists (*The Times*, 2 April 2004). Such is the level of concern that the British government suggested the introduction of rules to ensure that all imams coming into the UK should be able to speak English. Some commentators have pointed out that many members of the Muslim community in Britain feel that they are being persecuted and made to be scapegoats (*The Times*, 12 April 2004). As a result of this a new word 'Islamaphobia' has now entered the English language and is increasingly being used.

Projections of the growth of the Muslim community in Britain have also contributed to the debate about Islam. Migration Watch UK and the Institute for the Study of Islam and Christianity have estimated that the Muslim community may double by 2013 to between five and six million people. They argue that this increase, allied to the social problems that the Muslim communities face will result in a situation in which 'Britain will be unable to cope with and efficiently absorb such large numbers, creating uncontrollable tensions and fragmenting social cohesion' (Institute for the Study of Islam and Christianity, 2005: 14).

Within the South Asian community there is an increased sense of vulnerability, mainly among those of Indian background, and a worry that they may suffer from the reaction of White British people to those of other ethnic origins. Roy (2001) reported that some Indians no longer wanted to be described as Asian and early in 2002 the largest British Asian radio station, Sunrise Radio, announced that it would no longer use the term 'Asian' to refer to

Muslims, Hindus and Sikhs. This was in response to Indians who wanted to distance themselves from Islamic terrorists after 11 September 2001 (*Observer*, 26 May 2002).

1.3.5 The clash of Western and Asian cultures

In recent years the British media has featured a steady stream of negative stories about the South British Asian community, which have highlighted a number of cultural differences. For example, there have been stories about girls being forced into arranged marriages, and murders where girls have been killed because they have brought dishonour on their families by marrying someone out of their religious or racial group or by becoming pregnant outside of marriage. For example, in June 1995 Tasleem Begum was killed by her brother-in-law; in 1998 Rukhsana Naz was strangled by members of her family; in 2002 Heshu Yones had her throat slit by her father for seeing a Lebanese Christian man (*Observer*, 21 November 2004); and in December 2004 a Sikh man, Kalvinder Dosanjh, was jailed for fourteen years for hiring a contract killer to murder his daughter and her Jewish boyfriend since she had 'brought dishonour on her family' (*Guardian*, 16 December 2004).[11] In December 2004 the West Yorkshire Police announced that they were reopening the cases of 122 Asian women who had suspicious suicides or who had disappeared to see if they were linked with honour killings (*Guardian*, 16 December 2004). Despite the fact that such events are relatively rare, anecdotal evidence from members of the Asian community shows that many feel that they receive a disproportionate level of media coverage.

These five factors have raised the profile of religion, and particularly Islam, in the public consciousness and stimulated a debate about multiculturalism and immigration.

1.4 Does religion have any significance for young people growing up in Britain?

In recent decades some academics have argued that religion in the Western world has very little bearing on attitudes, if indeed any influence at all. This may be partly because some sociologists and social theorists espoused a theory of secularization which originated in the thinking of Weber (1965) and which has since been developed by a number of scholars.[12] Put simply, this theory has posited that in a post-enlightenment world science provides the key for understanding the world and human behaviour and consequently the practice and influence of religion is gradually and inexorably declining. While this theory has not been without its critics (for example, Bell, 1980: 328–32), it has been broadly accepted within many academic circles. However, whilst the decline in church attendance in the United Kingdom over the past century is well documented and is not in dispute (Currie, Gilbert and Horsley, 1977; Gill, 1993; Brierley, 2000; Graff and Need, 2000: 123), it is not clear that there is a decline in *all* forms of religion in the West, nor is it clear whether any decline is linear or part of a cyclical pattern.

There are three main factors that have raised questions about the theory of secularization. First, the growth of what are often called 'New Age' beliefs and practices (Gill, 1999: 79). Secondly, the persistence of relatively high levels of religious belief and practice in the United States of America, which arguably is the country most influenced by postmodernism and which does not seem to fit with a secularist theory (Stark and Bainbridge, 1985: 1–3; 1987: 279–313). Thirdly, a number of commentators have noted the worldwide resurgence of religion in the closing decades of the twentieth century, which appears to be not just a rise of fundamentalism among minority groups but a growth of what might be described as 'main stream religion' (Hammond, 1985; Newbigin, 1989: 212–13; Huntington, 1996: 95–101).

These, and other factors, have led some scholars to focus on the relative strength and persistence of religion in the modern world (Greeley, 1972; Stark and Iannaccone, 1994; Verweij, Ester and Nauta, 1997), whilst other scholars have re-examined the data and put forward alternative explanations. For example, some suggest that religion in the United Kingdom is not disappearing but, rather, changing and evolving. Davie, for example, commenting on the European Values Study, pointed out that the material tends to be clustered into two groups:

> On the one hand, those concerned with feelings, experience and the more numinous religious beliefs; on the other, those which measure religious orthodoxy, ritual participation and institutional attachment. It is, moreover, the latter (the more orthodox indicators of religious attachment) which display, most obviously, an undeniable degree of secularisation throughout Western Europe. In contrast, the former (the

less institutional indicators) reveal a considerable persistence in *some* aspects of religious life.

(Davie, 1994: 12)

Allied to theories of secularization has been the widespread assumption that religion has little or no effect on attitudes or behaviour. Gill (1999: 32–4), commenting on Christianity in Britain, traced the origin of this assumption back to research undertaken by Mass-Observation (1947), to Gorer's *Exploring English Character* (1955) and to some of the early Gallup Polls, which were used by Wilson (1966). However, Gill is critical of the definitions of churchgoing use by Mass-Observation and the way that Gorer confused empirical and moral statements that may have 'blurred moral differences between churchgoers and nonchurchgoers' (1999: 38).

Gill claimed that many theologians and sociologists have worked on a series of assumptions, namely that being a member of a congregation which meets for worship has 'little (beneficial) moral effect upon churchgoers' (1999: 2), that 'a review of literature within the sociology of religion over the last few decades does seem to confirm a widespread conviction that the beliefs and behaviour of churchgoers are little different from those of nonchurchgoers' (1999: 31) and that 'churchgoing is seldom thought to be an activity that has an appreciable effect upon moral/social attitudes or behaviour' (1999: 31). Gill has questioned the way that some scholars have interpreted the data and also pointed out that other polls (for example BBC, 1955, and ABC, 1965) showed a clear correlation between churchgoing and attitudes (Gill, 1999: 38–40). This has been backed up by a European Values Systems Study Group survey (Abrams, Gerard and Timms, 1985: 50–92), Francis (1982) and Francis and Kay (1995). Gill also examined data from the British Household Panel Surveys and the British Social Attitudes Surveys and concluded that

> The mass of new data shows that churchgoers are indeed distinctive in their attitudes and behaviour. Some of their attitudes do change over time, especially on issues such as sexuality, and there are obvious moral disagreements between different groups of churchgoers in a number of areas. Nevertheless, there are broad patterns of Christian beliefs, teleology and altruism which distinguish churchgoers as a whole from nonchurchgoers. It has been seen that churchgoers have, in addition to their distinctive theistic and christocentric beliefs, a strong sense of moral

order and concern for other people. They are, for example, more likely than others to be involved in voluntary service and to see overseas charitable giving as important. They are more hesitant about euthanasia and capital punishment and more concerned about the family and civic order than other people. None of these differences is absolute. The values, virtues, moral attitudes and behaviour of churchgoers are shared by other people as well. The distinctiveness of churchgoers is real but relative.

(Gill, 1999: 197)

These conclusions are backed up by the research that was undertaken by Roberts and Sachdev (1996: 107 and 110).

1.5 Listening to the voices of South Asian Britons

In assessing the importance of religion it is significant that a large proportion of those from ethnic minorities think that religion is very important and believe that religious categories are at least as important as ethnic categories in describing themselves. Modood, Beishon and Virdee (1994: 91), for example, asked the interviewees in their research how they wished to define themselves and concluded: 'Most South Asians, then, identified more with an ethnic or religious identity than with being "Asians".'[13]

The Fourth National Survey of Ethnic Minorities (Modood, 1997: 292–94) found that compared with the Caribbeans (who considered that skin colour was more important than religion in self-description) a higher proportion of the Indians, African Asians, Pakistanis, Bangladeshis and Chinese thought that religious categories were more important than skin colour to describe themselves. They concluded: 'Nationality continued to be stressed, but in the case of South Asians religion was held to be equally or more important' (Modood, 1997: 294). Other researchers have observed the same phenomenon.[14] The second reason was the value that many Asians placed on religion as an important influence in their lives. Not only do many South Asian British and African Asians choose to use religious categories to describe themselves, but compared with the white population a higher proportion consider that their religion is very important to them (Modood, 1997: 301).

1.6 Summary: growing up in Britain today

In this chapter I have outlined some of the changes in British society that are affecting young people today. I have described the decline in social capital and the concerns about immigration, asylum and the rise of Islam. I have also challenged the widespread view that religion has little relevance for young people today. In the chapter that follows we will listen to the young people themselves and ask: 'What can we know about the religious practices of young people growing up in Britain today?' I will then examine in some detail the religious practices of teenagers in contemporary Britain and see how their religious views affect and colour their attitudes towards a range of issues.

2
The religious affiliation and practices of teenagers in Britain

2.1 Introduction

It is commonly assumed that most white teenagers in Britain have little interest in religion. In contrast, there is a perception that young Blacks and Asians are more likely to be religious. For example, the media cites the growth of Black-led churches with gospel choirs as evidence of the emerging self-confidence of the Black community. Following the events of 11 September 2001 the media have also featured a number of stories of the growth of Islam especially among young Pakistanis and Bangladeshis, but also among black and white people.[1] At the same time an increasing number of Muslim women are wearing the burqha, and an increasing number of Sikh men are wearing the turban. Do the media's perceptions give us the whole picture? What can we discover if we listen to the young people themselves and ask them about their religions affiliation, practices and attitudes?

2.2 Religious affiliation

The 2001 UK census asked about religious affiliation, which is a useful comparator when we come to the affiliation of young people in Britain (table 2.1). It shows that 72 per cent of the population indicated that they were Christian, 23 per cent ticked either the 'no religion' box or did not give an answer, 3 per cent were Muslims and for each of the other religions there were fewer than 1 per cent.

Brook et al. (1992, Q-5), in a nationwide study, found that 74 per cent of young people claimed to be Christians and less than 1 per cent identified themselves as each of Hindus, Jews, Muslims and Sikhs. One quarter said that they did not have a religion. In Walsall, where the research for this book was undertaken, there was a relatively high proportion of other faiths (table 2.2). Some 61 per cent were Christians, 2 per cent were Hindus, less than 1 per cent were Jews, 8 per cent were Muslims and 6 per cent were Sikhs. A total of 21 per cent indicated that they had no religious affiliation (Smith, 2002: 55).

It is interesting to note that the vast majority (more than four-fifths) of the Walsall adolescents claimed that they belonged to one of the religious traditions, compared with the three-quarters of the teenagers in the Brook sample. What does this tell us? Certainly

Table 2.1 Religious affiliation: the 2001 UK Census

Religion	Number	Percentage
Christian	42,079,417	71.57
Buddhist	151,816	0.26
Hindu	558,810	0.95
Jewish	266,740	0.45
Muslim	1,591,126	2.71
Sikh	336,149	0.57
Other	178,837	0.30
No religion/religion not stated	1,3626,299	23.18

Source: http://www.statistics.gov.uk/census2001/profiles/uk.asp

Table 2.2 Walsall teenagers: Do you belong to a church or other religious group?

Religion	Number	Percentage
Christian	2,008	61
Buddhist	10	<1
Hindu	80	2
Jewish	2	<1
Muslim	276	8
Sikh	205	6
Hindu and Sikh	2	<1
Other unspecified	16	1
None	690	21

N = 3289

claims of affiliation are notoriously difficult to measure.[2] Are the respondents using the word 'Christian' in the sense of any good, upright citizen, rather than in the narrower sense of a specific religious allegiance? To what extent does this claim translate into behaviour, if at all? We need to look at specific religious practices and in particular at attendance at public worship to answer these questions.

2.3 Public worship

2.3.1 Attendance

Among the teenagers in Walsall, 51 per cent had attended worship in a church in the past year, 7 per cent had been to worship in a Sikh gurdwara, 8 per cent to a Muslim mosque and 5 per cent to a Hindu mandir (Smith, 2002: 56). These statistics reveal a gap of 10 percentage points between those who claim to be Christians (61 per cent) and those who had attended worship in a church in the previous year (51 per cent). The proportion of the teenagers who claimed allegiance to Islam and those who attended the mosque in the previous year was the same at 8 per cent. Of the sample, 6 per cent identified themselves as Sikhs, although 7 per cent claimed to have attended worship in a gurdwara in the previous year. And although 2 per cent called themselves Hindus, 5 per cent of the sample had attended worship at the mandir in the previous year. Overall more than seven out of ten (73 per cent) of the teenagers claimed to have attended worship in the previous year.

2.3.2 Frequency of attendance

The teenagers were asked about the frequency of attendance at worship (Smith, 2002: 58). A total of 16 per cent claimed that they attended nearly every week, 5 per cent at least once a month, 18 per cent 'sometimes' and another 18 per cent said that they went to church once or twice a year. In response to this question, 43 per cent indicated that they never attended a place of worship. A question was included about the regularity of attendance at worship at different ages (Smith, 2002: 58). Some 38 per cent had attended worship at least once a month when they were five to six years old, 42 per cent when they were nine to ten years old and 27 per cent when they were thirteen to fourteen years old. There was a small increase in attendance at worship between the ages of five to six and nine to ten, followed by a much larger decline by the time the adolescents were aged thirteen to fourteen.

2.3.3 Weddings and funerals

The adolescents were questioned about their attendance at weddings and funerals in the previous year and their responses reveal that 53 per cent had gone to a wedding and 28 per cent had attended a funeral at a place of worship (Smith, 2002: 57).

2.4 Personal spirituality

The young people were questioned about whether they prayed when they were alone (Smith, 2002: 59). In answer, 14 per cent said that they prayed every day, 7 per cent that they prayed at least once a week, 3 per cent prayed at least once a month and 29 per cent claimed to pray 'occasionally' when they were by themselves. Some 47 per cent stated that they never prayed alone. The overall picture we gain from these statistics is that whilst many of the adolescents attend worship for special occasions, it is only a minority who pray and attend worship on a regular basis.

The teenagers were also asked to respond to a statement about religious experience (Smith, 2002: 60). Some 66 per cent said they had not had a religious experience, 26 per cent were not sure and 8 per cent claimed that they had. Two-fifths of the adolescents did not think that their lives were being guided by God, 14 per cent thought they were being guided and 46 per cent responded either 'perhaps' or 'probably'. Only a small minority of the adolescents thought that they had had an experience of God's presence or leading (Smith, 2002: 61).

2.5 Summary

The majority of young people in Britain today (77 per cent) choose to use religious categories in their description of themselves. Only 23 per cent claimed to be non-religious or did not wish to state their religion. However, those who claim regular attendance at public worship form a much lower proportion than those describing themselves as belonging to a religion. Nevertheless, 51 per cent of the teenagers in Walsall still claimed to have attended worship in a church in the previous year, though this may be largely due to attendance at weddings and funerals. About a quarter of them prayed regularly. Levels of religious belief and practice in the United Kingdom are clearly not as high as they were in earlier decades. Nevertheless, it is equally clear that religion still plays a significant and regular part in the lives of many teenagers in Britain. In the following chapters we will look at the way that religion influences the attitudes of young people.

3
Well-being and mental health

3.1 Introduction

A sense of well-being comes from a variety of factors, such as good mental and physical health, wholesome personal relationships, financial security and living and working in a safe and secure environment. Worries are often expressed about the psychological health of the younger generation, especially in the more extreme cases when there is evidence of self-harm or attempted suicide. It is not rare to read stories in the media of teenage girls cutting themselves,[1] of the rise in teenage suicides among young men since the 1970s,[2] of the increase in anorexia and bulimia in young women,[3] and of the growing practice of prescribing antidepressants to young people.[4] The reasons for these trends are complex. Some have suggested that the rise in teenage male suicides is related to unemployment, divorce or to a crisis in male identity, exacerbated by the fact that girls of a similar age are now, on average, achieving higher examination results than boys. This is a particular cause of concern since suicide is the second highest cause of death among teenagers after road traffic accidents.[5] The rise in the incidence of anorexia and bulimia has been blamed on the obsession of the fashion industry with thin models. For many adolescents the teenage years are a time of inner turmoil, with periods of self-doubt alternating with periods of self-assurance and confidence. Many young people experience such mood swings which are part of the transition from childhood to adulthood as the teenager establishes his or her own identity, which may mean testing out the inherited views of one's parents and family, and making up one's own mind on issues.

In recent years there has been a growing interest in the connection between religion, well-being and happiness.[6] In this chapter

I set out to see if a connection can be found among adolescents, by posing the question: 'To what extent does religion influence the inner life of teenagers, their feelings and their sense of self-worth?' In order to obtain a benchmark we turn to Francis and Kay who asked six questions, examining the way that a group of the adolescents viewed themselves. Their responses are set out in table 3.1.

Some 45 per cent felt that their lives had a sense of purpose and 69 per cent found life really worth living. Only 13 per cent felt that they were not worth much as a person, while just over half often felt depressed (53 per cent). In response to the question 'I have sometimes considered taking my own life', 27 per cent agreed and 16 per cent thought that they tended to be lonely. These findings present us with a group of teenagers who were generally positive about themselves, yet with a significant proportion who sometimes felt depressed, experienced anxiety about what others thought about them and were sometimes jealous of others.

The same statements were put to the adolescents in Walsall, with an additional four, all of which explored different aspects of how they relate to other people (table 3.2).

It is striking how many of the teenagers were uncertain about whether their lives had a sense of purpose (55 per cent of the Francis and Kay group and 46 per cent of the Walsall group ticked 'not certain' or 'disagree'). Despite this, the majority of the young people in both groups felt positive about life and that it was really worth living (69 and 70 per cent respectively). Only a small proportion of each group experienced feelings of worthlessness (13 and 14 per

Table 3.1 Well-being: Francis and Kay

	Agree %	Not certain %	Disagree %
I feel my life has a sense of purpose	45	36	9
I find life really worth living	69	22	9
I feel I am not worth much as a person	13	23	64
I often feel depressed	53	18	29
I have sometimes considered taking my own life	27	16	57
I tend to be a lonely person	16	16	68

Source: Francis and Kay (1995: 44)

Table 3.2 Well-being: an overview of Walsall adolescents

	Agree %	Not certain %	Disagree %
I feel my life has a sense of purpose	55	35	11
I find life really worth living	70	20	10
I feel I am not worth much as a person	14	21	65
I often feel depressed	54	17	29
I have sometimes considered taking my own life	28	16	56
I tend to be a lonely person	14	12	74
What people think of me is important	73	13	14
I don't like being in large crowds	21	15	65
I like to have a lot of people around me	75	16	9
Sometimes I have been jealous of others	77	11	12

Source: Smith (2002: 66)

cent respectively). These findings contrast with the relatively large proportion that claimed that they often felt depressed (53 and 54 per cent respectively) and over a quarter who had thought about committing suicide (27 and 28 per cent respectively). About one in seven of the young people in both groups sometimes felt lonely (16 and 14 per cent respectively). In summary, a higher proportion of the Walsall adolescents were generally more certain about their feelings than the teenagers in the Francis and Kay research. More were positive about life and fewer were lonely. Nevertheless, a slightly higher proportion had low self-worth, became depressed and thought about suicide. Additionally, 73 per cent of the Walsall teenagers were concerned about what other people thought about them, 21 per cent did not like being in large crowds, 75 per cent liked to have a lot of people around them and 77 per cent were sometimes jealous of others.

3.2 The influence of Asian culture on well-being

The teenagers from Walsall were then divided into the White British group and the South Asian British group. Their responses are shown in table 3.3.

26 *Growing Up in Multi-Faith Britain*

Table 3.3 Well-being: the influence of Asian culture

	White British %	South Asian British %	χ^2	p<
I feel my life has a sense of purpose	54	60	8	.01
I find life really worth living	70	67	2	NS[7]
I feel I am not worth much as a person	14	17	4	.05
I often feel depressed	54	53	<1	NS
I have sometimes considered taking my own life	28	27	<1	NS
I tend to be a lonely person	13	17	5	.05
What people think of me is important	73	72	1	NS
I don't like being in large crowds	20	26	9	.01
I like to have a lot of people around me	75	77	1	NS
Sometimes I have been jealous of others	79	69	27	.001

Source: Smith (2002: 70)

Much research has been undertaken in the USA and Britain examining self-esteem, and a broad consensus has emerged that levels of self-esteem are broadly similar among adolescents in different ethnic groups.[8] However, among the Walsall adolescents there appear to have been some relatively small differences. Compared with the White British, a greater proportion of the South Asian British adolescents felt that life has a sense of purpose (60 per cent compared with 54 per cent). This may be due to a stronger sense of community and family solidarity in Asian communities; or it may be a result of the fact that they live in families who have made conscious decisions to migrate to another country; or it may be due to their religious or political beliefs. Yet, despite this, a greater proportion of the South Asian British teenagers experienced feelings of worthlessness (17 per cent compared with 14 per cent). The explanation for this is not obvious, although it may relate to being part of a minority which sometimes feels itself under threat, or even the higher levels of unemployment experienced by some sections of the South Asian British community.

A smaller proportion of the South Asian British teenagers experienced jealousy (69 per cent compared with 79 per cent).

Well-being and mental health 27

They included a larger proportion of lonely people (17 per cent compared with 13 per cent). This finding is surprising since the proportion of Asians who live alone is much smaller than in the white and black community (Modood, Beishon and Virdee, 1994: 32–3) and it might be assumed that fewer of them would feel lonely. The South Asian British teenagers also included a larger proportion who did not like being in large crowds (26 per cent compared with 20 per cent). Both of these statistics may reflect the experience of minority communities who are aware that their families have only arrived in Britain in recent decades and that in most parts of the country they are a small minority among a white majority population.

3.3 The influence of religion on attitudes towards well-being

We now turn to examine the effect that religious affiliation may have on the teenagers' sense of well-being. Table 3.4 sets out the responses of the adolescents when they were divided according to their religious affiliation and those whom I describe as non-affiliates (NA), that is those who indicated that they did not consider themselves to belong to any religious tradition.

3.3.1 Non-affiliates

A smaller proportion of the non-affiliates felt that their life had a sense of purpose (48 per cent) than those in the four religious groups, which was less than the average for all the Walsall teenagers (55 per cent) but more than those in the Francis and Kay group (45 per cent). This reveals that those who are practising members of a religion are more likely to believe that there is some sort of purpose and meaning in their lives than those who do not regularly attend worship. This may be due to their beliefs or it may be a result of the fact that people who attend worship get a sense of purpose by meeting with other like-minded people. Despite this, there were no significant statistical differences between the non-affiliates and those in the four religious groups when it came to how much they valued living, their sense of self-worth and any feelings of depression. Some 30 per cent of the non-affiliates had considered committing suicide, which was the same as the Hindu adolescents, but greater than the other religious groups. It was also

Table 3.4 Well-being: by religion

	Chr %	Hindu %	Muslim %	Sikh %	NA %	χ^2	p<
I feel my life has a sense of purpose	62	59	66	53	48	75	.001
I find life really worth living	72	64	68	67	70	4	NS
I feel I am not worth much as a person	14	13	19	16	13	7	NS
I often feel depressed	53	60	49	55	54	4	NS
I have sometimes considered taking my own life	25	30	24	29	30	10	.05
I tend to be a lonely person	14	21	16	16	13	7	NS
What people think of me is important	78	72	71	72	70	23	.001
I don't like being in large crowds	20	17	34	18	19	31	.001
I like to have a lot of people around me	75	77	74	81	75	4	NS
Sometimes I have been jealous of others	84	87	60	72	75	90	.001

Source: Smith (2002: 68)

a larger proportion than the Francis and Kay group (27 per cent) and the average for the Walsall teenagers (28 per cent). Stack (1991: 462–8) in a study in Sweden also found a correlation between religiosity and lower levels of suicides among the young (fifteen- to twenty-nine-year-olds). This is consistent with the finding that a smaller proportion of the non-affiliates thought that life had a purpose. They also had the smallest proportion who were lonely (13 per cent NS) and who were worried about what others think about them (70 per cent).

3.3.2 Christianity

The Christian adolescents in Walsall were the group with the highest proportion of those who really found life worth living (72 per cent NS), which was more than the Francis and Kay study

(69 per cent) and the average for the Walsall group (70 per cent). Compared with the other three religious groups a smaller proportion of the Christians experienced loneliness (14 per cent NS). In contrast, the Christians were also the group with the highest proportion who were anxious about what other people thought about them (78 per cent), which was 5 per cent more than the average. This may be due to the fact that it is not very cool for young people to admit that they are religious or it may be that teenagers who are anxious are more likely to join churches as places where they will receive a welcome and feel safe.

3.3.3   Hinduism

Compared with the other three religious groups a smaller proportion of the Hindu adolescents had low self-worth (13 per cent NS, the same as the non-affiliates). They were also the group with the smallest proportion who did not like being in large crowds (17 per cent), which was 4 percentage points less than the average. Conversely, a larger proportion of them often felt depressed (60 per cent NS). A larger proportion of them had sometimes considered suicide (30 per cent, the same as the non-affiliates), tended to be lonely (21 per cent NS) and had been jealous of other people (87 per cent, compared with the average for the Walsall teenagers of 77 per cent). It appears that more of the Hindus were worried about their lives and their relationships than those in the other three religious groups.

3.3.4   Islam

Examination of the feelings of Muslim young people presents an interesting picture, with widely contrasting attitudes. For example, a larger proportion of Muslims than any of the other groups felt that their lives had a sense of purpose (66 per cent). Yet at the same time a larger proportion also felt they were not worth much as a person (19 per cent NS).

The research also revealed that fewer of them felt depressed (49 per cent NS) than any other group and fewer had considered taking their own life (24 per cent). Of the four religious groups, a smaller proportion of the Muslims were concerned about what people thought of them (71 per cent), liked to have a lot of people around them (74 per cent NS) and experienced jealousy (60 per cent). Compared with all the other groups a larger proportion of them did not like being in large crowds (34 per cent). In summary, a larger proportion of the Muslim adolescents expressed contrasting and contradictory feelings than the other groups. For example, fewer were worried about what others thought about them and had been jealous of others, yet they were less likely to enjoy being with others in crowds.

It would be interesting to undertake more detailed personality profiling of young Muslims to see if any of these factors (in particular that a larger proportion of them had a sense of purpose and also feelings of personal worthlessness) may give some clues as to why a minority of young Muslims have been a fruitful recruiting ground for terrorist groups.

3.3.5 Sikhism
The adolescent Sikhs did not exhibit a very distinctive set of attitudes, although of the four religious groups a smaller proportion of the Sikhs felt that their lives had a sense of purpose (53 per cent, compared with the average of 55 per cent of the Walsall group) and a larger proportion of them liked to have a lot of people around them (81 per cent NS, compared with the average of 75 per cent of the Walsall young people).

3.4 Summary

Examining the young people of Walsall on the basis of their religious affiliation has thrown up some interesting and unexpected insights that would not have emerged if we had simply looked at their ethnic backgrounds. In particular it shows that people who hold religious beliefs are more likely to consider that life has a sense of purpose, are more concerned about what others think of them and are less likely to consider committing suicide. The exception to this is the group of adolescent Hindus who have the same proportion as the non-affiliates (30 per cent) of those who had considered taking their own lives. They also had the highest proportion who liked being with others and who were sometimes jealous. Perhaps the most distinctive set of attitudes were exhibited by the adolescent Muslims who had the largest proportion who felt that life has a sense of purpose and the lowest proportions who had considered suicide, who felt jealous of others and liked being in crowds.

4
Relating to other people

4.1 Introduction

In a survey in 2002 the telephone helpline for young people Get Connected found that 42 per cent of parents thought that the biggest problem that their teenagers faced was drugs. The teenagers themselves, however, saw things quite differently. 31 per cent of them said that their greatest worry was their relationships.[1] This illustrates the danger of not listening to the young people themselves. This is backed up by an article in *The Times* in June 1998 which reported a study entitled 'Hopes and Fears: Young European Opinion Leaders'. Five hundred fourteen- to twenty-year-olds were interviewed to find out what they wanted for the future. The overwhelming response was that 'they want to get married, have children and live happily ever after. They know it means putting their children first, sticking with their spouses even if they fall out of love, and protecting their families from the evils of infidelity and materialistic culture' (Brayfield, 1998: 19).

We have seen in the previous chapter that many young people are concerned about how they get on with others. We now explore this area further. Nine statements about relationships were put to the teenagers by Francis and Kay (1995) and their findings can be seen in table 4.1.

In response, 35 per cent of the adolescents indicated that they often wanted to get advice. Of the five groups of professionals mentioned, they were most likely to consult a youth leader (48 per cent), then a school teacher (46 per cent), a Christian minister (41 per cent), a social worker (40 per cent) and a doctor (32 per cent). When it came to friends and family, only 31 per cent of the young people took advice from their fathers. Far more of the adolescents found it helpful to chat with their mothers (51 per cent) and their close friends (61 per cent).

Table 4.1 Family and friends: Francis and Kay

	Agree %	Not certain %	Disagree %
I often long for someone to turn to for advice	35	26	39
I would be reluctant to discuss my problems:			
with a school teacher	46	28	26
with a youth club/group leader	48	30	22
with a doctor	32	34	34
with a Christian minister/vicar/priest	41	33	26
with a social worker	40	37	23
I find it helpful to talk about my problems:			
with my mother	51	19	30
with my father	31	23	46
with close friends	61	20	19

Source: Francis and Kay (1995: 15)

As an example of how fast youth culture is changing, it is interesting to note that there is now some evidence that young men in particular are turning to the Internet to find answers to their problems.[2] However, when the questionnaire was being assembled this possibility was not identified by any of the pilot groups. The responses of the Walsall teenagers to the same statements are set out in table 4.2.

A slightly greater proportion of the Walsall adolescents (36 per cent compared with 35 per cent) wanted someone to turn to for advice. As far as the professionals were concerned, smaller proportions of the Walsall adolescents were reluctant to turn to one of their school teachers (42 per cent compared with 46 per cent), a youth leader (41 per cent compared with 48 per cent), a Christian minister (34 per cent compared with 41 per cent) or a social worker (35 per cent compared with 40 per cent). This statistics reveal that the Walsall adolescents were generally happier to turn to professionals for advice than those in the Francis and Kay study. The only exception to this is in the case of a doctor. There are a number of possible explanations for the differences between the groups. It may be due to changes over time, since the

Table 4.2 Relationship with family and friends: an overview

	Agree %	Not certain %	Disagree %
I often long for someone to turn to for advice	36	27	37
I would be reluctant to discuss my problems:			
with a school teacher	42	29	30
with a youth club/ group leader	41	32	27
with a doctor	34	35	31
with a Christian minister/vicar/priest	34	35	31
with a social worker	35	36	29
I find it helpful to talk about my problems:			
with my mother	49	19	32
with my father	31	22	47
with close friends	66	17	17

Source: Smith (2002: 105)

Walsall research is more recent than the Francis and Kay work. It may also reflect that the young people in Walsall are from a uniformly urban area, whilst the Francis and Kay study reflects a much wider range of schools, including those situated in rural areas.

When we compare the statistics for friends and family we find that fewer of the Walsall adolescents found it helpful to talk about their problems with their mothers (49 per cent compared with 51 per cent). The responses to the statements about their fathers revealed that both group had almost identical attitudes (31 per cent). Other research has also confirmed that young people tend to find that their mothers are more empathetic than their fathers. In a much earlier study Eppel and Eppel (1966: 91) asked the adolescents what they did when they were in trouble. They found that the adolescents were more likely to turn to members of their family for help than to their friends. The adolescents in Walsall and in the Francis and Kay (1995) group appear to have placed a greater emphasis on turning to friends rather than to adults, although the questions were slightly different so comparison can only be made with caution.

4.2 The influence of Asian culture on attitudes towards family and friends

We now turn to look at the effect of ethnicity on the attitudes of the teenagers, which is set out in table 4.3. The data revealed some clear differences between the two groups. More of the South Asian British adolescents wanted advice (40 per cent compared with 35 per cent) and they were more likely to discuss their problems with professionals than the White British: with school teachers (43 per cent compared with 33 per cent), youth leaders (42 per cent compared with 32 per cent), clergy (35 per cent compared with 25 per cent) and social workers (36 per cent compared with 30 per cent). The exception was doctors, when the differences were not statistically significant (37 per cent compared with 34 per cent).

When it came to family and friends a smaller proportion of the South Asian British adolescents found it helpful to talk about their problems to their mothers (47 per cent compared with 50 per cent NS), their fathers (20 per cent compared with 32 per cent) and their close friends (64 per cent compared with 66 per cent NS).

Table 4.3 Attitudes towards family and friends: the influence of Asian culture

	White British %	South Asian British %	χ^2	p<
I often long for someone to turn to for advice	35	40	5	.05
I would be reluctant to discuss my problems:				
with a school teacher	43	33	18	.001
with a youth club/ group leader	42	32	21	.001
with a doctor	34	37	3	NS
with a Christian minister/vicar/priest	35	25	22	.001
with a social worker	36	30	7	.01
I find it helpful to talk about my problems:				
with my mother	50	47	1	NS
with my father	32	27	5	.05
with close friends	66	64	1	NS

Source: Smith (2002: 114)

At least some of these differences may be explained by the home situations in white and Asian households. Many South Asian British people live in extended households.[3] Not all of the teenagers appreciated this and the girls were especially critical (Saeed and Galbraith: 1981/2: 449).[4] There is some evidence that Asian parents, certainly in the past, have had more influence on their children than the parents of white teenagers (Beetham, 1967: 20).[5]

Brah (1979) looked at the levels of communication between Asian teenagers and their parents and found that there were a wide variety of experiences.[6] However, neither Brah's findings on the level of communication between teenagers and parents nor Anwar's report showing greater levels of respect for parents among Asian adolescents (Commission for Racial Equality Report, 1978: 18) were translated into a greater willingness of the Asian adolescents to discuss their problems with parents.

In another piece of empirical research, Stopes-Roe and Cochrane (1990: 143) surveyed a group of Hindus, Muslims, Sikhs and whites from the Birmingham area.[7] They found that more of the 'British' adolescents (95 per cent) turned to members of their household family than the Asian adolescents (86 per cent). There was not a very large difference between the Asian and 'British' adolescents when seeking advice from close family members (32 and 35 per cent respectively). However, when it came to 'family far' (that is, extended family) there was a large difference (16 per cent compared with 0 per cent respectively), which may be accounted for by the greater emphasis placed on the family by Asians.

When it came to talking through problems with their friends, Stopes-Roe and Cochrane (1990: 143) found that there was not a great difference between the Asian and the 'British' adolescents (53 and 50 per cent respectively). Among the Walsall adolescents a slightly greater proportion of the white group found it helpful to turn to friends (66 per cent NS), whilst a smaller proportion of the Asian group found it helpful (64 per cent NS).

In contrast to the results found in the research on Walsall teenagers, Stopes-Roe and Cochrane found that a slightly higher proportion of the 'British' adolescents turned to 'professionals' that the Asian adolescents (85 per cent compared with 82 per cent). It would have been interesting if Stopes-Roe and Cochrane had found out how often the Asian adolescents had turned specifically to social workers or to youth leaders since in the past this has been an area where there have been difficulties. One Community Relations Commission report claimed that 'Social workers who work in multi-racial areas reported that they most commonly find themselves facing problems in ethnic minority communities for which they feel themselves inadequately trained and prepared' (1977: 27). The report observed that 'It was also clear that ethnic minority youths were seldom able to make use of the conventional youth service because of the hostility of white young people. A fear of rejection leads to minority youth avoiding other agencies as well of youth clubs' (1977: 29). Tyler (1978: 36) claimed that 'There appears generally to be considerably less help [that is, counselling services] for young Asians, who may be suffering particularly severely from the conflicting demands of differing cultures'.

This brief look at the effect of ethnicity on the young people's need for help and their attitudes towards those who might offer it makes worrying reading for those involved in the support and nurture of South Asian British teenagers and raises questions about how this need can be better met. Although a greater proportion of them indicate that they want help, a smaller proportion of them are willing to seek it from professionals, family members and friends, when compared with the White British.

4.3 The influence of religion on attitudes towards family and friends

Having established that there are significant and important differences based on ethnicity, we now need to see if religious affiliation can shed any further light on these needs (table 4.4).

4.3.1 Non-affiliates

A smaller proportion of non-affiliates than in any of the religious groups wanted advice (33 per cent, compared with the average of 36 per cent). This might suggest a greater level of self-sufficiency or independence among the non-affiliates, which is consistent with the converse situation revealed in McGlone, Park and Roberts's research (1996: 69) which found that adults who were associated with a religion were more likely to seek advice. However, this research does not test why this is the case. Are anxious people more likely to turn to religion for help or does religious practice make a person realize that they might benefit from advice?

Table 4.4 Attitudes towards family and friends: by religion

	Chr %	Hindu %	Muslim %	Sikh %	NA %	χ^2	p<
I often long for someone to turn to for advice	39	42	40	40	33	16	.01
I would be reluctant to discuss my problems:							
with a school teacher	45	46	29	34	42	28	.001
with a youth club/ group leader	44	45	25	35	41	34	.001
with a doctor	36	45	36	36	32	12	.05
with a Christian minister/vicar/priest	35	35	22	24	36	26	.001
with a social worker	39	40	28	28	34	19	.001
I find it helpful to talk about my problems:							
with my mother	52	42	50	46	48	7	NS
with my father	33	27	28	26	32	6	NS
with close friends	70	67	63	65	64	12	.05

Source: Smith (2002: 109)

4.3.2 Christianity

Compared with the other three religious groups, a smaller proportion of the Christians (39 per cent) wanted advice. It might have been expected that the Christian adolescents would have been the least reluctant of all the groups to talk to a Christian minister, but this was not the case. The statistics also reveal that, compared with the average (table 4.2), the teenage Christians were more reluctant to speak to professionals and more likely to seek the advice of parents and friends.

4.3.3 Hinduism

A greater proportion of the Hindu adolescents wanted advice (42 per cent) than any other group. It is therefore surprising that of the four religious groups they were the most reluctant to discuss their problems with professionals, that is, 46 per cent were reluctant to discuss problems with a teacher, 45 per cent with a youth leader or a doctor and 40 per cent with a social worker. They were also the group that was most reluctant to talk to their mothers (42 per cent NS) and the second most reluctant to speak to their fathers (27 per cent NS). After the Christian adolescents they had the second greatest proportion who were keen to turn to their friends (67 per cent, compared with the average of 66 per cent). These figures suggest that a larger proportion of the adolescent Hindus worry than those in the other categories and that raises questions for professionals who are working with them. They appear to be a particularly vulnerable group and special training may be required for professionals to identify problems and to know how to respond to them.

4.3.4 Islam

A slightly higher than average (36 per cent) proportion of the young Muslims wanted advice (40 per cent). Of the five groups the Muslims were most willing to discuss their problems with professionals. It is particularly interesting that a smaller proportion were reluctant to turn to a Christian minister than the adolescent Christians (22 per cent compared with 35 per cent). However, of the four religious groups fewer Muslims found it helpful to discuss their problems with friends.

Much has been written about the Muslim way of life with its strong emphasis on the family. Traditionally Muslims have lived in extended households and the 2001 national census found that Muslims still live in the largest households in Britain.[8] This is especially true for those who originally came from the Indian subcontinent (Ballard, 1982: 181–3). At its best this communal lifestyle allows for the emergence of networks of pastoral care and friendship that can support young people in times of transition and need. Anwar's research (1994a: 25) led him to conclude that the vast majority of Muslims preferred to live in joint families, although the situation may be changing. As well as extended households, another significant factor in Muslim families is the distinctive role of women and girls. Many Muslim women do not go out to work and they will often spend much of their time together in each other's homes. Single girls tend live at home and in some cases are sent back to the family's country of origin to get married.[9] Afshar found considerable tensions in the relationships between mothers and daughters:

In all cases the break with the traditional concepts of familial unity and the close mother–daughter ties were broached with difficulty and were fraught with guilt and tensions. For the Muslim daughters the problem of accommodating contradictory public and private ideologies became virtually insoluble.

(1989: 213)

The mothers were more worried about bringing up their daughters than bringing up their sons.

This might lead one to presume that there would be a significant statistical difference between the Muslims and the Christians or non-affiliates with regard to finding it helpful to turn to their parents to discuss problems. However, this was not the case in Walsall. The adolescent Muslims did not exhibit a distinctive set of attitudes, other than that they were more likely to turn to their mothers for advice than their fathers, a phenomenon that was true of all five groups.

4.3.5 Sikhism

Of the four religious groups the Sikhs, after the Muslims, were the next most likely to turn to professionals, including Christian ministers. Turning to family relationships, Thompson, who was studying young Punjabi *Jat* Sikh men in Coventry, observed the strong sense of family and community and pointed out that none of them lived alone (1974: 244). Families normally included sons and their wives (p. 245). He also noted that most of the second-generation adolescents belonged to Punjabi peer groups:

> The peer groups give a framework outside the family for young people to maintain their Punjabi identity. The groups exert strong pressures on rebels, who are either forced to conform or are squeezed out, so that nearly all their links with their former friends are severed . . . The young second-generation boys who become rebels do not quickly pass a point of no return by, say, forgetting Punjabi completely, finally walking out of the joint family, or marrying an English girl.
>
> (p. 248)

It is interesting to compare the statistics of the Sikh adolescents with the average figures for the Walsall teenagers. The Sikhs were less likely to turn to their mothers (46 per cent NS compared with 49 per cent), fathers (26 per cent NS compared with 31 per cent) or close friends (65 per cent compared with 66 per cent).

4.4 Summary

The data confirms that teenagers are more likely to turn to their friends for advice than to their parents. However, when they do seek advice from a parent it is much more likely to be their mother than their father. My research also points to significant differences between the groups in Walsall, caused by both ethnic and religious factors. I have already pointed out that a greater proportion of South Asian British teenagers would like help but are less likely to seek it. Looking at the figures for the different religious groups we can see that this is a particular problem for young Hindus, many of whom want help but are finding it difficult to get. This contrasts with the adolescent Muslims of whom a smaller proportion want advice and yet they are more likely to seek it from professionals, parents and friends.

5
Sexual morality

5.1 Introduction

Young people growing up in Britain today are living in a world that is radically different from that of their grandparents. Although the majority of married people stay together, a significant number of marriages now end in divorce. Many teenagers are being raised in single-parent families or by people in a civil partnership. For them cohabitation rather than marriage is the norm. There has also been a revolution in sexual behaviour. Britain is reported to have the highest rate of teenage pregnancies in western Europe, with over 90,000 teenage girls becoming pregnant in 1997, of whom 8,000 were under sixteen years old and 2,200 were under fourteen years old (Ferriman, 1999). There has also been a rapid rise in sexually transmitted diseases. An article in *The Times* (31 March 2004), quoting a report from the Health Protection Agency, said that the number of new cases of sexually transmitted diseases in Britain among those under the age of twenty rose from 669,291 in 1991 to 1,332,910 in 2001. Other articles in *The Times* (2 June 2004 and 28 July 2004) gave further details, pointing out that:

> Gonorrhoea more than tripled in boys aged 13 to 19 between 1995 and 2002 and increased almost as rapidly in girls of the same age. Chlamydia quadrupled over the same period for teenage boys, rising to 234 cases per 100,000. It rose to almost 760 cases per 100,000 girls.

In November 2004 the government launched a £50m sexual health campaign which focused on young people. The Health Secretary, John Reid, commented that the problem had reached 'epidemic' proportions (*The Sunday Times*, 21 November 2004).[1]

Wilkinson and Mulgan (1995: 67) have charted some of the changes in sexual morality over recent decades. They show that there has been a sixfold rise in the divorce rate between 1961 and 1991; that first-time marriages are at their lowest level since 1889; and that those who marry are doing so at a later age. Scott, Braun and Alwin (1998: 27) found that 18 per cent of the 984 adults questioned thought that a married couple should stay together if they did not get along, even when there were no children. When they had children, 44 per cent thought that they should stay together. In a more recent study, Phillips found that when twelve- to nineteen-year-olds were asked the same question 66 per cent thought that the parents should stay together (Phillips, 2004: 58). Nearly half of the respondents (47 per cent) agreed that 'Divorce is usually the best solution when a couple can't seem to work out their marriage problems'.

There has also been a huge rise in cohabitation, which increased through most of the twentieth century (Gershuny and Brice, 1994: 40). Indeed, there is some evidence that cohabitation is now becoming the normative way of entering into marriage. Many people see this as a good thing because it enables couples to test whether or not they are compatible. However, evidence from the British Household Panel Survey shows that 'cohabiting couples were more than four times as likely to split as married couples' (Buck and Scott, 1994: 61–2). There has been a huge decline in the proportion of those who think that living together outside of marriage is always wrong. For example, before 1930 42 per cent of men and 35 per cent of women thought that cohabitation was wrong. For those born between 1960 and 1976 the proportion of those who think that cohabitation is wrong has declined to 8 per cent of men and 7 per cent of women (Buck and Scott, 1994: 75).

Bromley and Curtice (1999: 215) found that 59 per cent of the 235 respondents who were educated to degree or higher education standard thought that abortion should be allowed by law if a woman decides that she does not want to have children, whilst 58 per cent of the 361 respondents educated to intermediate level and 47 per cent of the 278 respondents questioned who had no educational qualification thought that abortion should be allowed. Turning to gay relationships, Ahrendt and Young found that in the general population there has been a decline in the proportion of those who think that sexual relations between adults of the same sex are always wrong from 1987 (74 per cent) to 1989 (69 per cent) to 1993 (64 per cent) (Ahrendt and Young, 1994: 86).

What do young people think about these trends? Research has shown that attitudes towards sexual and personal morality vary greatly between age groups and in different cultures (Inglehart, 1990: 194–211). Francis and Kay (1995) asked six questions (table 5.1). They found that 13 per cent thought that it was wrong to have sexual intercourse outside marriage and 24 per cent agreed that it was wrong to have sexual intercourse under the age of sixteen. One in five thought that divorce is wrong. And 5 per cent were against contraception, 38 per cent were against abortion and 39 per cent were against homosexuality. In each case a significant minority of the teenagers were uncertain about their views on these ethical matters (ranging between 17 and 30 per cent).

The same statements were put to the teenagers in Walsall (table 5.2). Their responses were broadly similar, although in response to the questions about sexual intercourse outside of marriage (16 per cent compared with 13 per cent) and under the legal age of sixteen years (28 per cent compared with 24 per cent), contraception (7 per cent compared with 5 per cent) and abortion (40 per cent compared with 38 per cent) they were slightly more conservative than those in the Francis and Kay research. Conversely, a marginally larger proportion expressed slightly more liberal views about divorce (with 55 per cent disagreeing that it was wrong compared with 54 per cent) and homosexuality (with 40 per cent disagreeing that it was wrong compared with 36 per cent). Phillips

Table 5.1 Sexual morality: Francis and Kay

	Agree %	Not certain %	Disagree %
It is wrong to have sexual intercourse outside marriage	13	17	70
Divorce is wrong	20	26	54
Contraception is wrong	5	23	72
Abortion is wrong	38	30	32
It is wrong to have sexual intercourse under the legal age (16 years)	24	22	54
Homosexuality is wrong	39	25	36

Source: Francis and Kay (1995: 83)

Table 5.2 Sexual morality: an overview

	Agree %	Not certain %	Disagree %
It is wrong to have sexual intercourse outside marriage	16	14	70
Divorce is wrong	19	26	55
Contraception is wrong	7	20	73
Abortion is wrong	40	27	33
It is wrong to have sexual intercourse under the legal age (16 years)	28	19	53
Homosexuality is wrong	38	22	40

Source: Smith (2002: 123)

(2004: 64) found that only 5 per cent of the twelve- to nineteen-year-olds thought that premarital sex is always wrong.

Turning to the subject of divorce, Inglehart (1990: 197) reported that 8 per cent of the fifteen- to twenty-four-year-olds in Britain thought that divorce could never be justified, which is a smaller proportion than either the Francis and Kay cohort (20 per cent) or the Walsall teenagers (19 per cent). The differences may, at least in part, be accounted for by the wording of the questions and may also reflect the changes in attitudes over time.

The attitude of young people towards homosexuality is also changing. In one study 31 per cent of the eighteen- to twenty-four-year-olds in Britain thought that homosexuality could never be justified (Inglehart, 1990: 194). Wellings et al. (1994: 248) asked a group of sixteen- to twenty-four-year-olds questions about gay sex. The responses showed that approximately 68 per cent of men and 52 per cent of women thought it was wrong for two men to have sex and approximately 62 per cent of men and 54 per cent of women thought it was wrong for two women to have sex together. In the Francis and Kay cohort and among the Walsall teenagers almost two-fifths thought that homosexuality was wrong.

5.2 The influence of Asian culture on attitudes towards relationships and sexual morality

The Francis and Kay study and the averages for the Walsall group allow us to some comparisons when we examine how ethnicity affects the teenagers' attitudes (table 5.3). The adolescents' responses reveal that the White British group was more liberal than the South Asian British group in all areas except in their views of homosexuality, where the statistics for those who thought it wrong were broadly similar, but statistically not significant (37 and 39 per cent respectively). The views of the two groups were most divided about sexual intercourse outside of marriage where 12 per cent of the White British teenagers thought it was wrong compared with 40 per cent of the South Asian British adolescents.

Divorce was disapproved of by 16 per cent of the White British teenagers compared with 35 per cent of the South Asian British. Ballard (1982: 192) noted that divorce was not usual in the Indian subcontinent and it was the duty of both families to help the couple sort out their problems. Asian families in Britain are also likely to get involved and to offer support or sanctions if there is any hint of marriage breakdown, since divorce means that the family loses honour (*izzat*). Brah (1978: 202; 1979: 261) discovered amongst her sample of Asian teenagers in Southall that they disapproved of

Table 5.3 Sexual morality: the influence of Asian culture

	White British %	South Asian British %	χ^2	p<
It is wrong to have sexual intercourse outside marriage	12	40	258	.001
Divorce is wrong	16	35	108	.001
Contraception is wrong	5	13	40	.001
Abortion is wrong	38	48	18	.001
It is wrong to have sexual intercourse under the legal age (16 years)	25	46	99	.001
Homosexuality is wrong	37	39	<1	NS

Source: Smith (2002: 134)

divorce strongly, although some of them referred to instances where the woman had remarried successfully.

The two groups expressed different views about contraception. Some 5 per cent of the White British group felt that it was wrong compared with 13 per cent of the Asian group. Wellings et al. (1994: 341) asked about the sort of contraceptives used and found that people who identified themselves as religious were less likely to use contraception than those of 'no religion'. However, within the religious group there was considerable variation of practice between the Christian and the non-Christian group in their use of different methods of contraception.

As far as abortion was concerned Wellings et al. (1994: 257) found that 38 per cent of the White British group disapproved of abortion compared with 48 per cent of the South Asians.

Finally, there was a gap of 21 percentage points between the two groups of Walsall teenagers when questioned about their attitudes on sexual intercourse under the legal age (25 per cent of the White British group thought it was wrong compared with 46 per cent of the South Asian British). Wellings et al. (1994: 54) asked their sample if they had first had sexual intercourse under the age of sixteen and found that a smaller proportion of the Pakistani, Bangladeshi and Indian group (11 per cent of the men and 1 per cent of the women) compared with the white (20 per cent of the men and 8 per cent of the women) and black people (26 per cent of the men and 10 per cent of the women) had done so. The Wellings research shows that there are significant difference between males and females and the responses of the Walsall adolescents may hide similar differences; as Ballard contended:

> Girls are under stricter surveillance than boys, for it is felt that too much freedom might spoil a girl's reputation and thus damage her chances of making a good marriage. In addition the status and prestige of the family as a whole depends upon keeping its reputation, much of which rests with the chaste behaviour of its women, irreproachable.
> (Ballard, 1979: 117)

5.3 The influence of religion on attitudes towards relationships and sexual morality

How do the differences between the South Asian British and the White British compare when we turn to religious affiliation?

Research undertaken among adults suggests that there may be some differences. For example, Wellings et al.'s research among adults found that

> Those affiliated to no religious denomination are less likely to disapprove of premarital sex (only 2.6% men and 3.8% women in this group do so), those of Christian faiths other than Anglican or Roman Catholic (mainly Baptist) more likely to do so (20.3% men and 22.0% women), and those of non-Christian religious affiliation very much more likely to do so (46.2% of men and 41.3% women believe premarital sex to be always or mostly wrong).
>
> (1994: 248)

Is there any evidence that teenagers have the same attitudes? The adolescents in Walsall were asked about their religious allegiance and their answers reveals how religion affects their attitudes concerning issues of sexual morality (table 5.4).

5.3.1 Non-affiliates

The non-affiliates displayed some of the most liberal views about sexual morality. For example, it was the group with the smallest proportion who thought that it was wrong to have sexual intercourse outside of marriage (10 per cent compared with the average of 16 per cent) and under the legal age (20 per cent compared

Table 5.4 Sexual morality: by religion

	Chr %	Hindu %	Muslim %	Sikh %	NA %	χ^2	p<
It is wrong to have sexual intercourse outside marriage	15	23	56	26	10	361	.001
Divorce is wrong	19	15	49	26	14	181	.001
Contraception is wrong	5	4	21	6	6	93	.001
Abortion is wrong	44	25	62	39	35	86	.001
It is wrong to have sexual intercourse under the legal age (16 years)	31	40	57	33	20	177	.001
Homosexuality is wrong	37	22	53	26	38	46	.001

Source: Smith (2002: 126)

with the average of 28 per cent). Phillips found that those who did not belong to a religion have distinctive liberal attitudes. For example, 92 per cent of those who did not belong to a religion thought that it was all right for a couple to live together before marriage, compared with 71 per cent of those who belong to a religion; 29 per cent of non-religious people compared with 45 per cent of religious people though that under-age sex is always wrong; and 1 per cent compared with 13 per cent thought that pre-marital sex was always wrong (Phillips, 2004: 61 and 66). The non-affiliates were also the group with the smallest proportion who thought that divorce is wrong (14 per cent compared with the average of 19 per cent). Turning to issues of contraception and abortion, out of the five groups, they had the most liberal views after the Hindu teenagers.

5.3.2 Christianity

Compared with the other three religious groups a smaller proportion of the Christians thought that sexual intercourse outside of marriage was wrong (15 per cent) and that sexual intercourse under the legal age was wrong (31 per cent). In a much earlier piece of research Schofield found that teenagers who came from a church going family were less likely to have had sexual intercourse at an early age (1965: 71).

In response to the statement that 'homosexuality is wrong' the adolescent Christians in Walsall were broadly similar to the average for all the Walsall adolescents (37 per cent and 38 per cent respectively agreed) and the survey of teenagers by Francis and Kay (39 per cent agreed).

5.3.3 Hinduism

Of the four religious groups the Hindu teenagers had the smallest proportion who thought that divorce was wrong (15 per cent compared with the average of 19 per cent). Hinduism has traditionally taught that divorce is wrong (Hiro, 1972: 9; Brah,1978: 202) although in some circumstance Hindu men have been allowed to remarry (Jackson and Killingley, 1991: 19). Warrier (1994: 195) pointed out that the situation is complicated by caste, since 'Prajapatis accept the legitimacy of both divorce and widow-remarriage, both of which are shunned by higher-caste Gujaratis as violations of Brahmanical codes of morality'. Despite the traditional teaching of the Hindu faith, Khera noted the growing phenomenon of single-parent families in Southall (1981: 107).

A smaller percentage of Hindu adolescents agreed with the statement 'Contraception is wrong' than any other group (4 per cent), which reflects the lack of official Hindu teaching on the subject (Henley, 1983a: 52). However, Jackson and Killingley (1991: 20) pointed out that some streams of Hinduism teach that the only purpose of sexual intercourse is procreation.

Hindus tend to disapprove of abortion, although it is not uncommon (Henley, 1983a: 53; Jackson and Killingley, 1991: 20). This research found that a smaller proportion of Hindu adolescents disapproved of abortion (25 per cent) than any of the other groups, including the non-affiliates. Compared with the other four groups, fewer of the teenage Hindus thought that homosexuality was wrong (22 per cent). After the Muslim adolescents (57 per cent) the Hindus had the second highest proportion (40 per cent) who thought that it was wrong to have sexual intercourse under the legal age.

Apart from their views on sexual intercourse under the legal age, the general picture of the Hindu adolescents is that they had more liberal views on sexual morality than any of the other three religious groups and in some cases more liberal than the non-affiliates.

5.3.4 Islam

The proportion of Muslims who thought that it is wrong to have sexual intercourse outside marriage (56 per cent) was more than twice that of Sikhs (26 per cent) and nearly four times that of the Christians (15 per cent). Whilst the Quran forbids sex outside of marriage (Darsh, 1984: 5; Sarwar, 1992: 8; Hewitt, 1993: 16), Brown (1970: 135) claimed that in the early days of immigration when many of the young Pakistani men had come to work in Britain without their families, it was not unusual for them to resort to prostitutes, and Butterworth pointed out that 'Figures, for example, for venereal disease and the number of children born to local women and Pakistani fathers indicate that many were living with or otherwise involved with local-born women' (1969: 147). More recently, Raza has acknowledged that sexual activity outside marriage is not uncommon among Muslim teenagers (1993: 58).

In Walsall, 49 per cent of the Muslim adolescents thought that divorce was wrong. Hashnie (1967: 5) claimed that divorce is disapproved of in Islam, although in exceptional circumstances it is allowed but only after reconciliation has been tried (Hewitt, 1993: 19). The general view is that it is considered shameful if a woman divorces and in the sight of other Muslims she loses *izzat* (Wilson, 1978: 104–5). Afshar (1989: 214–16) found that divorced Muslim Pakistani women had faced considerable opposition and even rejection by their families. Surprisingly, Hiro (1991: 147) thought that in the Indian subcontinent divorce was more common among Muslims than among Hindus and Sikhs. This was certainly not reflected in the attitudes of the Walsall adolescents.

With regard to contraception, a greater proportion of Muslim adolescents thought it was wrong compared to other groups. Even so, the figure was surprisingly low at 21 per cent, which is probably because there is no specific teaching on the subject in the Quran. Omran's (1992: 225–38) view was that in certain limited situations Islam allows the use of contraception. Henley (1983c: 49) noted that some Muslims preferred not to use contraceptives since they thought that it was against nature. Hewitt claimed it was not allowed except when the health of the mother is at risk (1993: 26). However, Baraitser (1999: 138) found that none of the twenty Muslim or three Sikh women who were interviewed in Glasgow 'felt that their religion had any bearing on the use of contraception by married women'.

The proportion of Muslims who thought that abortion was wrong (62 per cent) was higher than in all the other groups, despite there being no universally held view of abortion in Islam. Omran (1992; 191–2) described the opinions of eight Islamic schools, and noted that all of them had different rulings. This was reflected in the views of individual British Muslims, although a majority were against abortion.

Muslims are taught that it is wrong to have sexual intercourse under the legal age (Sarwar, 1994: 10), although in practice the situation may be different. Joly noted:

> The treatment accorded to boys and girls is also different. Parents are more lenient to boys who may go through a phase which, if known to parents, would attract their disapproval. They go to cafés, play with fruit machines, drink, smoke, go to discos, have girl friends and generally 'hang around'. They thus lead a double life. Some got up to a great deal of mischief, yet behaved perfectly well at home . . . Girls generally do not and cannot follow this pattern.
>
> (1995: 167)

Shaw found a similar situation among some of the Pakistani families in east Oxford (1988: 173–4). Some 57 per cent of the adolescent Muslims in Walsall thought that it was wrong to have sexual intercourse under the legal age, which was a greater proportion than any other group and more than twice the proportion of adolescents nationally (Francis and Kay, 1995: 83).

The traditional Muslim teaching is that homosexuality is wrong (Sarwar, 1992). However, only 53 per cent of the teenage Muslims reflected this teaching in their response to the question, showing that young Muslims do not necessarily follow the teaching of the imams.[2] Again this was the greatest proportion of any of the five groups questioned.

In conclusion, we see that in response to all six questions a higher proportion of the Muslim adolescents compared with any other group thought that liberal sexual behaviour was wrong. Of all the groups they had the most distinctive profile concerning sexual behaviour. This is in line with the sentiments expressed by Siddiqui (1990: 13), when he quoted 'One of the goals of the Muslim Community in Britain', which was 'To develop the Muslim community as an island of peace, harmony and moral excellence, free of promiscuity, sexually transmitted diseases, drinking, gambling, drug-addiction, fornication and the related social and moral disorders which plague our age . . .'.

5.3.5 Sikhism

In the 1970s Thompson (1974: 245–6) studied second-generation Punjabi boys in Coventry. He found that the good reputation of these boys was very important if they were to be married to Punjabi girls and therefore they were not expected to have sex before marriage. However, this piece of research demonstrated that only 26 per cent of the Sikh adolescents thought that sex outside marriage was wrong. This was a smaller proportion than the Muslims, but greater than the Hindus, Christians and the non-affiliates.

After the Muslims the Sikh adolescents had the second highest proportion who thought that divorce was wrong (26 per cent). In the Sikh scriptures marriage is considered to be indissoluble. However, in practice Sikhism allows the remarriage of divorcees when a marriage has irretrievably broken down (Kohli, 1974: 55).

The Sikh religion does not forbid contraception (Henley, 1983b: 44). Ballard (1979: 126) quoted the example of a young Sikh woman who used contraception and the frustrations of the older Sikh women who were waiting for her to get pregnant. Simons found that 'almost 80% of the Sikhs report the practice of some form of birth control' (1982: 176). He concluded that 'Sikhs are now inclined to have families of moderate size at most. They resemble the general population in the practice of birth control: a majority use modern methods and these are now adopted early in marriage' (p. 173). This is in line with findings from this research that only 6 per cent of the Sikh adolescents thought contraception was wrong.

Henley argued that Sikhs disapprove of abortion (1983b: 44), although only 39 per cent of the adolescents in Walsall thought that abortion was wrong. One third of the adolescent Sikhs in Walsall thought that it was wrong to have sexual intercourse under the legal age, which is higher that the average for the young people in the research by Francis and Kay (24 per cent). This is a smaller proportion than Walsall Hindus (40 per cent) and Muslims (57 per cent). And 26 per cent of the Sikhs thought that homosexuality was wrong, which was a smaller proportion than the teenagers in the Francis and Kay research (39 per cent) and apart from the Hindus (22 per cent) was the smallest proportion of the groups in the Walsall findings.

5.4 Summary

Analysis of the sexual mores of teenagers has yielded some of the greatest contrasts in our survey so far. When the statistics were examined on the basis of ethnicity we found that in every case the South Asian British teenagers were more conservative in their views than the White British. When we delved further and looked at the differences between the different religious groups a more nuanced picture emerged. The adolescent Hindus had views which were more liberal than the other three religious groups and in some cases were more liberal than the average for the whole group. Conversely, the adolescent Muslims exhibited the most distinctive profile of all the groups, showing that they held the most traditional views on sexual morality. It is interesting to note that the Hindu (22 per cent) and Sikh (28 per cent) teenagers had the lowest proportions that thought that homosexuality was wrong, lower than the non-affiliates (38 per cent) and the average for the White British (37 per cent). For those involved in health education and the prevention of sexually transmitted diseases these results indicate that it may be advisable to focus resources and health campaigns, on the basis not of ethnicity, but of religious affiliation.

6
Questions of right and wrong

6.1 Introduction

There is concern in society about the perceived increases in crime, as evidenced by stories in the media about violence, road rage and mugging. Some of these worries have been generated by a series of high-profile cases, which have served to highlight and exacerbate widespread unease about crime among young people, notably, the murders of Stephen Lawrence in 1993, Damilola Taylor in 2000, Letisha Shakespeare and Charlene Ellis in 2003, and Anthony Walker in 2005. At the same time there is evidence to show that the levels of crime committed by young people are increasing. The 2004 Offending, Crime and Justice Survey found that 26 per cent of the population aged between ten and twenty-five had been involved in some sort of crime.[1]

In parallel with this there is some data that shows that respect for the law and for the police force has declined. The 1985 Gallup Survey of Britain found that 48 per cent of the general public thought that the police were efficient and did their job well (Heald and Wybrow, 1986: 266). However, research undertaken more recently by Tarling and Dowds (1997: 205) showed that there is a considerable lack of trust towards the police, with only 51 per cent trusting the police not to bend the rules 'just about always' or 'most of the time', 35 per cent thinking that they would not bend the rules 'only some of the time' and only 10 per cent thinking that they 'almost never' bend the rules. To what extent are the views of adults about crime, violence and policing echoed by young people today? Francis and Kay (1995: 98) put seven statements to the adolescents in their research (table 6.1).

Only 7 per cent thought that there was nothing wrong with shoplifting, 19 per cent with travelling without a ticket, 15 per cent

Table 6.1 Right and wrong: Francis and Kay

	Agree %	Not certain %	Disagree %
There is nothing wrong in:			
shoplifting	7	8	85
travelling without a ticket	19	24	57
cycling after dark without lights	15	10	75
playing truant from school	18	19	63
buying cigarettes under the legal age (16 years)	27	16	57
buying alcoholic drinks under the legal age (18 years)	39	20	41
writing graffiti wherever you like	16	19	65

Source: Francis and Kay (1995: 98)

with cycling after dark without lights, 18 per cent with playing truant, 27 per cent with buying cigarettes under the legal age, 39 per cent with buying alcoholic drinks under the legal age and 16 per cent with writing graffiti, indicating that the majority of the young people were fairly law abiding, apart from the underage purchase of alcohol. The same statements were put to the teenagers in Walsall, along with four additional statements (table 6.2).

The responses of the Walsall teenagers to the statements on shoplifting, travelling without a ticket, playing truant and graffiti were broadly similar to those in the Francis and Kay cohort. A larger proportion of the Walsall adolescents thought that it is wrong to cycle after dark without lights (19 per cent compared with 15 per cent), to buy cigarettes (32 per cent compared with 27 per cent) and to purchase alcoholic drinks under the legal age (44 per cent compared with 39 per cent). Some 31 per cent claimed that they had never stolen anything, although over half (55 per cent) admitted to stealing. And 11 per cent claimed that they had never told a lie. Wilkinson and Mulgan noted a growing preparedness to break the law:

> There is also some evidence that younger generations have become more willing to protest. Public tolerance for illegal demonstrations has risen

Table 6.2 Right and wrong: an overview

	Agree %	Not certain %	Disagree %
There is nothing wrong in:			
shop-lifting	8	9	83
travelling without a ticket	18	28	55
cycling after dark without lights	19	13	68
playing truant from school	17	17	66
buying cigarettes under the legal age (16 years)	32	18	50
buying alcoholic drinks under the legal age (18 years)	44	19	37
writing graffiti wherever you like	16	21	64
I have never stolen anything in my life	31	14	55
I have never told a lie	11	4	85
Sometimes I have taken advantage of people	60	24	16
The police do a good job	44	21	35

Source: Smith (2002: 139)

over the last decade with 68 per cent now agreeing that there are times when protesters are justified in breaking the law, an increase of 14 per cent since 1984.

(1995: 104)

Six out of ten of the Walsall adolescents admitted that they had sometimes taken advantage of other people.

A total of 44 per cent thought that the police do a good job. This ambivalence towards the police is in line with the research quoted earlier in the chapter (Heald and Wybrow, 1986; Tarling and Dowds, 1997).

6.2 The influence of Asian culture on attitudes towards right and wrong

Some interesting differences emerged when the cohort was divided into White British and South Asian British (table 6.3). In response to each of the statements the South Asian British group showed themselves to have more law-abiding attitudes than the White

Table 6.3 Right and wrong: the influence of Asian culture

	White British %	South Asian British %	χ^2	p<
There is nothing wrong in:				
shop-lifting	8	6	3	NS
travelling without a ticket	18	15	4	.05
cycling after dark without lights	20	13	13	.001
playing truant from school	17	15	2	NS
buying cigarettes under the legal age (16 years)	34	21	36	.001
buying alcoholic drinks under the legal age (18 years)	47	25	89	.001
writing graffiti wherever you like	16	14	2	NS
I have never stolen anything in my life	32	30	<1	NS
I have never told a lie	11	11	<1	NS
Sometimes I have taken advantage of people	61	57	3	NS
The police do a good job	44	42	1	NS

Source: Smith (2002: 146)

British adolescents. They were also more law abiding than the average for all Walsall adolescents (table 6.2) and those in the Francis and Kay study (table 6.1). However, eight out of the twelve responses were statistically not significant, so caution must be exercised when drawing conclusions.

Research shows that some parts of the South Asian British community lack confidence in the police. Saeed and Galbraith asked 100 Asian teenagers to respond to the statement 'The police in this country are busy catching criminals and do their job well'. They found that 69 per cent agreed, 17 per cent disagreed, 9 per cent neither agreed nor disagreed and 5 per cent did not know (1981/82: 452). Anwar (1998: 91) reported that the results of a 1983 survey on police protection among 570 young Asians revealed that only 15 per cent thought the level of police protection was good, 42 per cent thought it was average, 24 per cent said it was poor and 12 per cent did not know. It must be a cause of concern for the police that teenagers express so little confidence in them, not least because in the past concern has been expressed about the lack of racial diversity in the police and attempts have been made to recruit more officers form ethnic minorities.

6.3 The influence of religion on attitudes towards right and wrong

Roberts and Sachdev undertook research into the degree to which religion might be a factor in preventing crime. They found that 6 per cent of the adolescents in their study thought that religion would be 'very effective' in preventing crime and 26 per cent thought that religion would be 'quite effective' in helping prevent crime. They concluded: 'Taking religion more seriously is not regarded as an effective means of crime prevention: 66% thought that this would not be very or not at all effective compared with 32% who thought it would be very or quite effective' (1996: 87). However, they also found that those who were religious were more likely to think that belief in God would be a factor in discouraging people from committing crimes (p. 88). What does an examination of the responses of the Walsall adolescents reveal when they are divided into the four religious groups and the non-affiliates? Their responses to the statements are shown in table 6.4.

6.3.1 Non-affiliates

The non-affiliates revealed a distinctive set of attitudes in response to the first seven statements, which involved issues of obeying the law. In each case it showed that a higher proportion of the non-affiliates thought there was nothing wrong in breaking the law compared with those who had a religious affiliation, with the Francis and Kay research and with the average response for the whole Walsall group.

6.3.2 Christianity

Compared with the other three religious groups a higher proportion of the Christian adolescents thought that there was nothing wrong with buying cigarettes under the legal age (29 per cent compared with the average of 32 per cent) and in buying alcoholic drinks under the legal age (42 per cent compared with the average of 44 per cent). Although the average for all the White British teenagers

Table 6.4 Right and wrong: by religion

	Chr %	Hindu %	Muslim %	Sikh %	NA %	χ^2	p<
There is nothing wrong in:							
shoplifting	6	4	6	7	10	19	.001
travelling without a ticket	15	12	15	15	20	15	.01
cycling after dark without lights	16	10	16	11	23	41	.001
playing truant from school	13	4	18	15	20	38	.001
buying cigarettes under the legal age (16 years)	29	17	21	23	38	61	.001
buying alcoholic drinks under the legal age (18 years)	42	35	17	32	51	127	.001
writing graffiti wherever you like	13	6	13	18	19	24	.001
I have never stolen anything in my life	30	32	35	24	33	8	NS
I have never told a lie	8	4	14	10	13	23	.001
Sometimes I have taken advantage of people	60	67	48	64	61	19	.001
The police do a good job	52	39	50	33	39	59	.001

Source: Smith (2002: 143)

who thought that 'The police do a good job' was 40 per cent, when analysed in more depth the statistics showed that this comprised 39 per cent of the non-affiliates and 52 per cent of the Christians.

6.3.3 Hinduism

In their responses to the first seven statements, the Hindu group of adolescents had the smallest proportion who agreed with breaking the law, apart from buying alcoholic drinks under the legal age: thus shoplifting (4 per cent), travelling without a ticket (12 per cent), cycling without lights (10 per cent), playing truant (4 per cent), buying cigarettes under the legal age (17 per cent) and writing graffiti (6 per cent). They were also the group with the smallest proportion who said that they had never told a lie (4 per cent). A larger proportion appear to be more honest and law abiding than any of the other groups. Despite this, more of them (67 per cent) admitted taking advantage of people than in any other group.

6.3.4 Islam

Compared with the other three religious groups the adolescent Muslims in Walsall had the highest proportion who thought that there was nothing wrong in playing truant (18 per cent) and the smallest proportion who thought there was nothing wrong in buying alcohol (17 per cent) under the legal age. A higher proportion than any other group claimed that they had never stolen (35 per cent NS) and had never told a lie (14 per cent). Fewer of them claimed to have taken advantage of others (48 per cent).

A leading article in *The Times* (3 September 1999) claimed that the number of Muslims in prison had doubled in six years. In 1990 there had been 1,840 Muslims in prison, but in 1999 this had increased to 4,355. In 2003 the total had reached 6,095.[2] Despite this, the Muslim adolescents had the second highest proportion (after the Christian teenagers) who thought that the police do a good job. This may reflect the innate respect for authority that Islam seems to produce. It may also be significant that some police forces have tried especially hard to engage with the Muslim community. For example, Joly (1987: 73) noted that some Pakistanis in Birmingham had representation on the Police Liaison Committees and that 44 per cent of mosques in Birmingham sent delegates to their local Police Liaison Committees (Joly, 1995: 79).

6.3.5 Sikhism

Compared with the other three religious groups there was a higher proportion of Sikh adolescents who thought that there was nothing wrong in shoplifting (7 per cent) and in writing graffiti (18 per cent). However, they had the smallest proportion who claimed that they had never stolen anything (24 per cent NS) and the smallest proportion who thought that the police do a good job (33 per cent).

6.4 Summary

The comparison of the responses based on ethnicity revealed that there were striking differences between the White British and the South Asian British youngsters, showing that the latter considered themselves to be more law abiding than the former. This was most notable in their attitudes to buying alcohol and cigarettes under the legal age. When comparisons were made on the basis of religion it revealed that those with a religious affiliation were more likely to be law abiding than the non-affiliates. Of all the five groups the Hindus expressed the greatest respect for the law.

7
Substance use and abuse

7.1 Introduction

Although the vast majority of adults in Britain have taken soft drugs in the form of tobacco or alcohol, compared with the young generation a much smaller proportion have taken cannabis or hard drugs.[1] This may explain, at least in part, why the media spends so much time on the use of drugs by teenagers, especially teenage girls.[2] One high-profile example is Leah Betts who took an ecstasy tablet at her eighteenth birthday party in November 1995 and died later after drinking too much water in an attempt to counteract the effects of the drug; another is that of Katie Walsh, a sixteen-year-old from Swindon, who died of a drug overdose in January 2004. Under the headline of 'Britain's coolest city has worse drug-death toll', the *Observer* (3 November 2002) claimed that at least one person died in Brighton each week due to a drug overdose. Although such tragedies are relatively rare (and kill far fewer people than lung cancer, alcoholism or traffic accidents) these stories receive a disproportionate amount of coverage.

Whilst there has been a decline in the number of people who smoke tobacco in recent years, the use of alcohol and hard drugs has increased significantly. Gould, Shaw and Ahrendt (1996: 93) have pointed out that 'The number of registered drug addicts has increased from around 1,000 in 1970 to almost 30,000 in 1993, whilst seizures of drugs by customs and the police have risen from 11,000 in 1974 to nearly 70,000 in 1992', and 'In 1993 around three in ten (thirty-one per cent) of sixteen year olds were found to have used an illegal drug'. In answer to a question in the House of Commons on 30 March 2001 it was estimated that there were about 266,000 drug addicts in the UK. In 2005 it was reported that, among fifteen-year-olds in Europe, British youth were the heaviest cannabis users.[3]

In response to these worries the government and the police have launched a number of initiatives. For example, in 1998 Keith Hellawell was appointed as 'Drugs Tsar' and given the task of halving the availability and use of cocaine and heroin by young people. In 2000 Scotland Yard redirected their resources against the use of narcotics by deciding not to arrest people for possessing cannabis. In 2002 three of the four government's national targets were dropped and instead the police were asked to concentrate on reducing the use of Class A drugs by the under twenty-fives. In 2003 the Serious Organised Crime Agency announced that they were planning to fight the largest drug traffickers. In 2004 cannabis was downgraded and police were directed to combat medium-size drug traffickers (*The Times*, 26 November 2004). At the same time the use of drug treatment orders has been widened.

Francis and Kay put five statements to adolescents (table 7.1) to explore their attitudes substance use and abuse. They found that the vast majority was against glue sniffing (81 per cent) and the use of heroin (79 per cent). A total of 58 per cent thought it wrong to use cannabis, 22 per cent to become drunk, and 45 per cent to smoke cigarettes.

When the same statements were put to the teenagers in Walsall the results shown in table 7.2 emerged. In response to four of the five statements a smaller proportion of the Walsall adolescents compared with those in the Francis and Kay study indicated that they agreed: 75 per cent thought it was wrong to sniff glue, 42 per

Table 7.1 Substance use: Francis and Kay

	Agree %	Not certain %	Disagree %
It is wrong to sniff glue	81	6	13
It is wrong to use marijuana (cannabis, hash or pot)	58	19	23
It is wrong to become drunk	22	17	61
It is wrong to smoke cigarettes	45	17	38
It is wrong to use heroin	79	10	11

Source: Francis and Kay (1995: 112)

Table 7.2 Substance use: an overview of Walsall adolescents

	Agree %	Not certain %	Disagree %
It is wrong to sniff glue	75	10	15
It is wrong to use marijuana (cannabis, hash or pot)	42	29	30
It is wrong to become drunk	23	17	60
It is wrong to smoke cigarettes	39	18	43
It is wrong to use heroin	66	16	18

Source: Smith (2002:148)

cent were against the use of cannabis, 39 per cent thought it was wrong to smoke cigarettes and two-thirds were against the use of heroin. Only in their attitude towards smoking cigarettes was the proportion of Walsall teenagers higher (1 percentage point more).

Attitudes toward drunkenness have changed dramatically in recent years. For example, Cox (1967: 149) asked a group of sixth-formers about their attitude towards drunkenness and smoking. He found that 95 per cent of the boys and 97 per cent of the girls thought that it was 'always, usually or sometimes wrong' to get drunk. This change may be due to the significant rise in consumption of alcohol among young people in recent decades (Silbereisen, Robins and Rutter, 1995: 534). However, Cox discovered that 58 per cent of the boys and 57 per cent of the girls thought that it was 'always, usually or sometimes wrong' to smoke. It is interesting to note that attitudes towards alcohol had changed much more dramatically than attitudes towards smoking cigarettes.

However, attitudes towards drugs are also changing. Between 1983 and 1995 the proportion of those who thought that cannabis should be legalized increased. But, 'Only a third of the under-25s believe that cannabis should remain illegal, compared with over two-thirds of those aged 45 or above' (Gould, Shaw and Ahrendt, 1996: 96). This compares with 30 per cent of the Walsall adolescents and 23 per cent of the teenagers in Francis and Kay who did not think that it was wrong to use cannabis. In a more recent study of sixteen- to twenty-five-year-olds, 57 per cent of the young men and 62 per cent of the young women wanted the use of ecstasy to be illegal, but only 24 per cent of the men and 26 per cent of the women wanted the use of cannabis to be illegal (Henderson, 1998: 20).[4]

These results reveal the extent to which the Walsall teenagers were less worried about substance use than the adolescents in the Francis and Kay study.

7.2 The influence of Asian culture on attitudes towards substance use and abuse

Nazroo (1997: 30) studied the smoking and drinking habits of adults, based on their ethnicity. The differences between the South Asians and the White British were marked. Of the South Asians 15 per cent smoked cigarettes and 17 per cent had smoked in the past. This compared with 36 per cent of the white group who were currently smoking and 61 per cent who had smoked at one time. Further, 72 per cent of the South Asian British people had never drunk alcohol and only 14 per cent drank alcohol once a week or more. This contrasted with 13 per cent of the White British group who had never drunk alcohol and 56 per cent who drank once a week or more.

How does this compare with teenagers? We turn to the Walsall adolescents and divide the sample into the White British and the South Asian British (table 7.3) in order to examine the effect of culture on the attitudes of the adolescents. The differences in the

Table 7.3 Substance use: the influence of Asian culture

	White British %	South Asian British %	χ^2	p<
It is wrong to sniff glue	75	75	1	NS
It is wrong to use marijuana (cannabis, hash or pot)	42	39	2	NS
It is wrong to become drunk	18	50	252	.001
It is wrong to smoke cigarettes	37	50	30	.001
It is wrong to use heroin	66	67	1	NS

Source: Smith (2002: 154)

66 *Growing Up in Multi-Faith Britain*

responses of the two groups to sniffing glue, using cannabis and heroin were virtually identical but were not statistically significant. However, there were significant differences in the response of the White British group who thought that becoming drunk (18 per cent) and smoking cigarettes (37 per cent) was wrong compared with those from a South Asian British background, where 50 per cent of the adolescents thought that they were wrong. These findings are consistent with the data obtained from the research among adults by Nazroo (1997).

7.3 The influence of religion on attitudes towards substance use and abuse

Francis and Mullen (1993: 669) have shown that religion affects adolescents' attitudes towards drugs. Cochrane and Sukhwant (1990: 759) also found a clear association between alcohol use and religion in their study of Hindu, Muslim, Sikh and white men in Birmingham. They found that the group which was most likely to be regular drinkers were the Sikhs, followed by the whites and then the Hindus. Only a small number of Muslim men drank regularly, but paradoxically on average they consumed the most alcohol.

When the teenagers in Walsall were divided into the four religious groups and the non-affiliates, the influence of their religious views on their attitudes emerges clearly (table 7.4).

7.3.1 Non-affiliates

The non-affiliates in the study had the lowest proportion who thought it was wrong to become drunk (15 per cent) and to smoke cigarettes (34 per cent). These were lower than the average figures for the Walsall teenagers (table 7.2) and those in the Francis and Kay cohort (table 7.1).

7.3.2 Christianity

Compared with the other religious groups the adolescent Christians in the group had the lowest proportion who thought it was wrong to become drunk (22 per cent) and, equal with the Sikhs, the lowest proportion who thought it was wrong to smoke cigarettes (42 per cent).

Table 7.4 Substance use: by religion

	Chr %	Hindu %	Muslim %	Sikh %	NA %	χ^2	p<
It is wrong to sniff glue	78	85	73	73	74	11	.05
It is wrong to use marijuana (cannabis, hash or pot)	50	51	38	35	37	51	.001
It is wrong to become drunk	22	31	70	30	15	387	.001
It is wrong to smoke cigarettes	42	53	55	42	34	58	.001
It is wrong to use heroin	72	73	71	60	61	43	.001

Source: Smith (2002: 150)

7.3.3 Hinduism

Traditional Hinduism has taught that it is wrong to use tobacco, alcohol or other drugs (Henley, 1983a: 51). However, there is a wide variety of practice within the Hindu community concerning substance use. For example, it is rare for Gujurati men to smoke or drink, but not unusual to find Punjabi men who go to pubs and are used to drinking alcohol and to smoking tobacco (Knott, 1986: 36; Vertovec, 1996: 79). The Valmikis, a caste that draws on elements of both Hinduism and Sikhism, do not forbid the drinking of alcohol (Nesbitt, 1994: 139), whereas members of the Hare Krishna movement eschew all stimulants. No attempt to differentiate between forms of Hinduism was made so one must be aware that the data on Walsall teenagers gives only a general picture of all Hindus. It shows that the Hindus were the group with the greatest proportion against sniffing glue (85 per cent), cannabis (51 per cent) and heroin (73 per cent). When it came to alcohol only 31 per cent thought that it was wrong to become drunk. The results show that significant numbers of Hindus were against the use of substances.

7.3.4 Islam

Islam teaches that Muslims are not supposed to take any sort of drugs (Hewitt, 1993: 32). Indeed, it is widely presumed by proponents of Islam that no practising Muslim could conceive of taking drugs. For example, in the *Newsletter of the National Association of Young Muslims* (7, 1986) it is stated that 'There is no evidence yet that Muslim young people are involved in that [drug taking, particularly heroin] to an alarming extent . . . Only one case has come to our knowledge'. The article went on to encourage Muslim youth organizations to inform young people of the dangers and described a number of warning signs that might indicate when someone was taking drugs. However, anecdotal evidence shows that many young Muslims do in fact take drugs and these findings show that the Muslim and Sikh adolescents had the lowest proportion of teenagers who thought it was wrong to sniff glue (73 per cent).

Islam similarly forbids the drinking of alcohol. Even if a drop of alcohol is used in cooking it makes it unlawful (*haram*) to eat the food. Most orthodox Muslims would not admit to drinking alcohol and it would be disapproved of by many. Despite this, some Muslims do drink alcohol (Saifullah-Khan, 1974: 318; Wilkinson, 1988: 20–1). Not surprisingly, 70 per cent of the adolescent Muslims in the survey thought that it was wrong to become drunk. There is no specific prohibition on smoking in the Quran, so it is surprising that the Muslim teenagers have the highest proportion of all the groups who thought that it was wrong to smoke cigarettes (55 per cent).

7.3.5 Sikhism

The Sikh religion also forbids the use of substances. Nevertheless, with Muslims, the Sikhs had the lowest proportion of the religious groups who thought that it was wrong to sniff glue (73 per cent) and the lowest proportion compared with all other groups who thought it was wrong to use cannabis (35 per cent) and heroin (60 per cent).

Sikhism is against the drinking of alcohol (Henley, 1983b: 43). Despite this, Ghuman (1980: 314) found that most of the Bhattri Sikh men in Cardiff went to the pub or drank alcohol at home and there is widespread evidence to support this.[5] In Walsall only 30 per cent of the Sikh adolescents thought that it was wrong to become drunk.

Smoking is strongly disapproved of by Sikhs.[6] Drury (1988: 204; 1991: 395 and 1996: 101) found that none of the Sikh girls in her study smoked cigarettes. However, among the Walsall Sikhs only 42 per cent of the adolescents surveyed thought that it was wrong to smoke cigarettes.

7.4 Summary

Ethnicity has been found to be an important indicator of attitudes towards substance use, with the South Asian British being less likely to smoke or get drunk. Religion has also emerged as a key indicator about attitudes to various forms of substance use. Of all the groups, the Hindus are less likely to sniff glue and the Muslims are less likely to smoke cigarettes or get drunk. The group which was least worried about cigarettes and drunkenness was the non-affiliates.

8
Free time and leisure pursuits

8.1 Introduction

It is not uncommon to hear the complaint that young people spend too much time watching television or playing computer games. The revolution in information technology has increased the amount and type of entertainment available and there has been a rapid growth in communication and computing. Bill Clinton observed that when he became President of the USA in 1993 there were fifty registered websites on the Internet. Seven years later there were around 350 million websites (Clinton, 2001). Today computers are a requirement even in playgroups for pre-school children and most young people take it for granted that they can communicate instantaneously around the world using e-mail. Whereas more than half of the under twenty-fives use the Internet, only one in twenty people aged over sixty-five use it (Gardner and Oswald, 2001: 168). At the same time teenagers are far more likely to own and use a mobile phone than older people. Even the way that young people use the mobile phone is different, since they tend to send text messages, a system used far less by older people.

The way that many young people spend their time today contrasts with the traditional pursuits of former generations, when a far higher proportion of teenagers belonged to uniformed organizations, sports clubs, local authority youth clubs and church youth clubs. Francis and Kay put eight statements to the adolescents about leisure (table 8.1).

A total of 67 per cent indicated that they regularly spend time with friends without being involved in any particular activities. This is not a new phenomenon. Some years earlier Willmott (1966: 28) found that 52 per cent of the fourteen- and fifteen-year-olds in his study said that the main activity in their free time was

Table 8.1 Leisure: Francis and Kay

	Agree %	Not certain %	Disagree %
I often hang about with my friends doing nothing in particular	67	10	23
In my area there are lots of things for young people to do in their leisure time	27	16	57
I wish I had more things to do in my leisure time	58	15	27
I am frightened of going to a youth centre	8	16	76
My youth centre is boring	34	42	24
My parents prefer me to stay in as much as possible	17	18	65
My parents allow me to do what I like in my leisure time	49	17	34
My parents do not agree with most of the things that I do in my leisure time	28	18	54

Source: Francis and Kay (1995: 125)

'hanging about' or 'larking about'. Some 27 per cent of the teenagers in Francis and Kay's study thought that there were plenty of recreational activities for young people, yet 58 per cent regretted the lack of things to do in their spare time, and a small minority (8 per cent) were frightened of going to the youth centre. One third (34 per cent), however, were bored with the youth centre, which may explain why they did not use it. Around 17 per cent of the teenagers indicated that their parents preferred them to stay in as much as possible, whilst 49 per cent claimed that their parents allowed them to do what they liked in their free time. Just over a quarter (28 per cent) thought that their parents disapproved of what they did in their leisure time.

The same statements were put to the teenagers in Walsall and their responses are shown in table 8.2. The responses to the first statement were exactly the same in both groups. However, the differences in responses to the other statements were quite striking. A smaller proportion of the Walsall adolescents thought that there were plenty of leisure activities in the locality (19 per cent compared

72 *Growing Up in Multi-Faith Britain*

Table 8.2 Leisure: an overview of Walsall adolescents

	Agree %	Not certain %	Disagree %
I often hang about with my friends doing nothing in particular	67	10	24
In my area there are lots of things for young people to do in their leisure time	19	16	65
I wish I had more things to do in my leisure time	64	13	23
I am frightened of going to a youth centre	12	19	69
My youth centre is boring	44	39	18
My parents prefer me to stay in as much as possible	27	18	55
My parents allow me to do what I like in my leisure time	47	17	37
My parents do not agree with most of the things that I do in my leisure time	34	20	46

Source: Smith (2001: 160)

with 27 per cent) and a larger proportion wished they had more to do in their recreational time (64 per cent compared with 58 per cent). More of the Walsall adolescents were frightened of going to youth centres (12 per cent compared with 8 per cent) and thought that they were boring (44 per cent compared with 34 per cent). The perceptions of the Walsall adolescents about parental attitudes also showed a number of differences. A larger proportion of the Walsall parents wanted their teenagers to stay at home (27 per cent compared with 17 per cent). Fewer of them thought that their parents allowed them to do what they liked (47 per cent compared with 49 per cent). The proportion of the Walsall teenagers who agreed with the statement 'My parents do not agree with most of the things that I do in my leisure time' was 6 percentage points higher.

Overall, we see that the teenagers in Walsall were not as satisfied about the opportunities and facilities as the young people in the Francis and Kay cohort, and the responses to the last three statements show that a higher proportion of the Walsall teenagers felt that their parents were more restrictive.

8.2 The influence of Asian culture on attitudes towards leisure

The responses of the Walsall adolescents were divided into the White British and the South Asian British group (table 8.3). More of the White British teenagers hung around with their friends doing nothing (69 per cent) than the South Asian British young people (55 per cent), and 8 per cent fewer of them thought that there were plenty of things for young people to do in the locality. Taylor, Evans and Fraser found that a smaller proportion of adolescent Asians went to 'town' on a weekly basis and that they were far more likely to identify strongly with their local area (1996: 213).[1] A larger proportion of the White British young people thought that the youth centre was boring (47 per cent compared with 29 per cent), although other research has showed that South Asian British young people are less likely to go to a local authority youth club than white adolescents (but more likely to belong to a sports club).[2]

Table 8.3 Leisure: the influence of Asian religion

	White British %	South Asian British %	χ^2	p<
I often hang about with my friends doing nothing in particular	69	55	38	.001
In my area there are lots of things for young people to do in their leisure time	18	26	21	.001
I wish I had more things to do in my leisure time	63	68	3	NS
I am frightened of going to a youth centre	12	12	<1	NS
My youth centre is boring	47	29	57	.001
My parents prefer me to stay in as much as possible	23	54	215	.001
My parents allow me to do what I like in my leisure time	49	35	34	.001
My parents do not agree with most of the things that I do in my leisure time	33	42	15	.001

Source: Smith (2002: 172)

The South Asian British young people thought that their parents were more directive and that they allowed them less freedom. The proportion of the South Asian British who said that their parents preferred them to stay at home was 31 percentage points greater and the proportion of the parents who did not agree with the things they chose to do in their free time was 9 percentage points greater. A smaller proportion of them were given freedom in their spare time by their parents (35 per cent compared with 49 per cent). Other researchers have also observed that Asians are more likely to socialize in family group and around religious activities.[3] The situation for South Asian girls is quite different from that of boys and it is much less usual for girls to be allowed to go to youth groups (Hasnie, 1977: 27).

8.3 The influence of religion on attitudes towards leisure

The sample of young people was broken down into the four religious groups and the non-affiliates and the results are shown in table 8.4.

8.3.1 Non-affiliates

Compared with the four religious groups more of the non-affiliates hung around with their friends (70 per cent), were bored by youth centres (47 per cent) and were given freedom by their parents (50 per cent). Fewer of them wanted more things to do in their free time (62 per cent NS) and said that their parents wanted them to stay in (22 per cent). In other words they were the group that was given the greatest amount of freedom and yet they were also the most critical of the facilities and opportunities that were available for them.

8.3.2 Christianity

A larger proportion of the Christian adolescents than any of the other three religious groups hung around with their friends (67 per cent), thought the youth centre was boring (46 per cent) and claimed that their parents allowed them to do what they liked in their recreation time (47 per cent). Fewer of them thought that there were plenty of things for young people to do (18 per cent,

Table 8.4 Leisure: by religion

	Chr %	Hindu %	Muslim %	Sikh %	NA %	χ^2	p<
I often hang about with my friends doing nothing in particular	67	62	50	59	71	49	.001
In my area there are lots of things for young people to do in their leisure time	18	21	31	23	18	27	.001
I wish I had more things to do in my leisure time	66	69	70	64	62	9	NS
I am frightened of going to a youth centre	13	9	11	14	11	3	NS
My youth centre is boring	46	28	26	32	47	59	.001
My parents prefer me to stay in as much as possible	24	46	55	55	22	220	.001
My parents allow me to do what I like in my leisure time	47	37	37	32	50	38	.001
My parents do not agree with most of the things that I do in my leisure time	29	32	44	42	36	33	.001

Source: Smith (2002)

which was the same proportion as the non-affiliates), that their parents preferred them to stay in (24 per cent) and thought that their parents did not agree with how they used their leisure time (29 per cent). This profile of the Christian adolescents is closer to the profile of the non-affiliates than to any of the other three religious groups.

8.3.3 Hinduism

The Hindu adolescents did not present a particularly distinctive profile when compared with the other groups, apart from the fact that a smaller proportion of them were frightened of going to a youth centre (9 per cent NS) than any other group. Only 21 per cent thought that there were plenty of things for young people to do in the area.[4] In many areas the Hindu community has a tradition of arranging activities for their young people (Knott, 1986: 50; Hiro, 1991: 156; and Warrier, 1994: 208).

8.3.4 Islam

Compared with the other groups, fewer of the Muslim teenagers hung around with their friends (50 per cent) and were bored by the youth centre (26 per cent). Conversely, a larger proportion of the adolescent Muslims in Walsall thought that there were plenty of things for young people to do in the area (31 per cent). These figures suggest that a larger proportion of the Muslim adolescents were purposeful in their attitude to free time. Part of the reason for this may be that much of the social life of a typical Muslim is centred on the family (Livingstone, 1977) and the mosque (Dickinson et al., 1975: 137). The Islamic community has also been active in organizing activities.[5] Despite various organized activities, a larger proportion of the Walsall Muslims than the other religious groups wished they had more things to do in their spare time (70 per cent NS), more of them thought that their parents preferred them to stay in as much as possible (55 per cent, the same proportion as the Sikhs) and more said that their parents did not approve of their recreation activities (44 per cent). Part of this may be due to the attitudes of their parents and the imams, some of whom condemn what others would consider to be commonplace leisure activities, such as music,[6] dancing (Jeffery, 1976: 96 and 93; and Sarwar, 1994: 14) and going to the cinema (Lewis, 1996: 7).

In the Commission for Racial Equality's report (1978: 37) Hindu, Muslim and Sikh adolescents were asked if they would like more freedom than their parents gave them. They found that a smaller proportion of the Muslim adolescents wanted more freedom than they were given, compared with the Hindus and Sikhs.

8.3.5 Sikhism

Like the Muslims, there is a strong sense of family life in the Sikh community (Ballard, 1972/3: 19–21), which can restrict the freedom of their young people. Compared with the other three religious groups a smaller proportion of the Sikh adolescents wished there were more leisure activities available (64 per cent NS) and compared with the other four groups a smaller proportion thought that their parents allowed them to do what they liked in their free time (32 per cent).

More of them were frightened of going to the youth club (14 per cent NS) than in any other group and 55 per cent said their parents preferred them to stay at home (the same proportion as the Muslim group), which was greater than the other groups.

Like the Muslim community, the Sikh community focuses a great deal of social life around its place of worship; the gurdwara, and regularly organizes social and sporting activities for young people.[7] One of the factors behind the large proportion of young people who said that their parents preferred them to stay at home is the way that many Sikh families discourage their daughters from going out (Kalra, 1980: 64). Drury (1996: 103) found that a majority of the girls in her study disliked the lack of freedom, not least because the boys were not placed under similar restrictions.

8.4 Summary

When examining the effect of ethnicity, we found that the South Asian British parents were far more likely to limit the amount of time spent on social activities and also to influence the type of social activities of their teenage children. The adolescents themselves were more positive about spare-time activities and opportunities than were their White British counterparts and wished they had more time for leisure.

When we look at the influence of religion we can see that the teenagers who came from the religious groups were more likely to be purposeful in their use of recreational time and to be less critical of facilities and the opportunities that were available. The Hindu, Muslim and Sikh adolescents' spare time was more likely to be influenced by their parents and they were also more positive about the range of activities available.

9
Education and schools

9.1 Introduction

Education in Britain is rarely out of the political spotlight. Changes in policy and debates about priorities and educational methods are frequently in the media. Some of these are good news stories, such as the annual reporting of examination results. For example, the results of the Standard Assessment Tests (SATs) for seven-, eleven- and fourteen-year-olds across England and Wales have generally improved, more young people have passed GCSEs and A levels, and the average grades of passes have risen year by year. As a corollary of this, increasing numbers of young people are choosing to continue their education by going on to university. Young people in Britain today, it is claimed by some, are more educated than in any previous generation.

However, at the same time the media also presents many negative views. A cursory reading of the newspapers may suggest that, although there are good exam results, our education system is in serious crisis. There have been some high-profile cases, reported in the media, of parents being sent to prison because their children were truanting persistently. The genuine quality of academic achievement is questioned. Each August when the GCSE and A-level results are published, there is a public debate about whether educational standards are actually rising or whether the exams are simply getting easier. In 2003 worries about education and educational standards were illustrated by a Channel Four television series in which thirty GCSE students were prepared for, and sat, 1950s O-level papers. At the beginning of the series the pupils were set an exam, which they presumed was a 1950s GCSE paper. Much was made of the fact that most of them performed badly and it was then revealed that the exam was, in fact, a 1950s eleven-plus paper.

Francis and Kay (1995) put eight statements concerning school and teachers to the teenagers (table 9.1). More than seven out of ten (71 per cent) indicated that they were happy in their school and 90 per cent liked the people they went to school with. Nearly two-thirds (66 per cent) were worried about their school work, with just over one-third (35 per cent) finding school boring. A total of 73 per cent were worried about school exams and one quarter were worried about being bullied. More than two-fifths (42 per cent) were positive about their teachers and 67 per cent thought that school was helping to preparing them for life.

The young people in Walsall were asked the same questions (table 9.2). Five of the responses were almost exactly the same as those in the Francis and Kay research. In both groups 71 per cent indicated that they liked their schools. This is similar to the findings of other reseach.[1] More of the Walsall young people thought that school was boring (42 per cent compared with 35 per cent). Furnham and Gunter's research (1989: 168) discovered that, in response to the statement 'I get bored and fed up with school and do not really enjoy anything connected with it', 39 per cent agreed and 34 per cent disagreed, which is broadly similar to the Walsall and the Francis and Kay teenagers.

The proportion of the Walsall young people who were worried about being bullied was 7 percentage points greater and the proportion who thought that the teachers were doing a good job

Table 9.1 School: Francis and Kay

	Agree %	Not certain %	Disagree %
I am happy in my school	71	18	11
I like the people I go to school with	90	7	3
I often worry about my school work	62	17	21
School is boring	35	23	42
I am worried about my exams at school	73	14	13
I am worried about being bullied at school	25	23	52
Teachers do a good job	42	31	27
My school is helping to prepare me for life	67	21	12

Source: Francis and Kay (1995: 32)

Table 9.2 School: an overview of Walsall adolescents

	Agree %	Not certain %	Disagree %
I am happy in my school	72	15	13
I like the people I go to school with	90	6	4
I often worry about my school work	64	13	23
School is boring	42	20	38
I am worried about my exams at school	73	12	15
I am worried about being bullied at school	32	19	49
Teachers do a good job	47	27	27
My school is helping to prepare me for life	67	19	14

Source: Smith (2001: 179)

was 5 percentage points greater (47 per cent compared with 42 per cent). Furnham and Gunter (1989: 168) asked a more general question about teachers' teaching ability and found that, in response to the statement 'Teachers are good at getting their ideas across in the classroom', just over one-third agreed.

Just over two-thirds (67 per cent) in both groups felt that their school was helping to prepare them for life. In 1994 the Department for Education and Employment (1996: 22) asked a group of sixteen-year-olds about their attitude to school. In response, 42 per cent thought that their school had done little to prepared them for life (which is a larger proportion than in Walsall), although the proportion of pupils who felt this had been declining annually. They also found that 8 per cent of the teenagers thought school had been a waste of time.

9.2 The influence of Asian culture on attitudes towards school

The Christians and non-affiliates were compared with the Hindu, Muslim and Sikh adolescents (table 9.3). The proportion of the South Asian adolescents who were happy in their school was 6 percentage points greater than in the White British group. More of them worried about their schoolwork (72 per cent compared with 63 per cent), exams (87 per cent compared with 71 per cent) and being bullied (38 per cent compared with 30 per cent). The

Table 9.3 School: the influence of Asian culture

	White British %	South Asian British %	χ^2	p<
I am happy in my school	71	77	9	.01
I like the people I go to school with	90	89	<1	NS
I often worry about my school work	63	72	18	.001
School is boring	45	29	43	.001
I am worried about my exams at school	71	87	61	.001
I am worried about being bullied at school	30	38	13	.001
Teachers do a good job	45	53	11	.001
My school is helping to prepare me for life	66	71	6	.05

Source: Smith (2002: 186)

proportion of them who thought that school was boring was 17 percentage points smaller. They were more positive about their teachers (53 per cent compared with 45 per cent) and that school was helping them to prepare for life (71 per cent compared with 66 per cent). In summary, the South Asian British teenagers were more positive about education and their school than the white teenagers. These findings are backed up by other research.[2] They also have higher academic aspirations.[3] Research also shows that adolescent Asians have higher levels of academic success at both 'higher grade' and A levels than their black or white contemporaries and that greater proportions stayed on to study full time.[4]

9.3 The influence of religion on attitudes towards school

Education is a major concern for the South Asian British community, who have campaigned for years to have their own schools, a right which has now been granted.[5] However, the vast majority of South Asian British adolescents are still being educated in state schools and their views are important if we are to understand some of the issues that particularly concern them. The four religious groups were compared with the non-affiliates and their responses are shown in table 9.4.

Table 9.4 School: by religion

	Chr %	Hindu %	Muslim %	Sikh %	NA %	χ^2	p<
I am happy in my school	76	86	81	70	68	41	.001
I like the people I go to school with	91	94	88	89	90	3	NS
I often worry about my school work	69	81	69	74	59	54	.001
School is boring	38	22	27	35	49	81	.001
I am worried about my exams at school	77	90	86	87	66	101	.001
I am worried about being bullied at school	34	36	40	37	28	29	.001
Teachers do a good job	56	51	60	46	39	99	.001
My school is helping to prepare me for life	72	71	70	74	62	40	.001

Source: Smith (2002: 184)

9.3.1 Non-affiliates

A smaller proportion of the non-affiliates were happy in their school and were worried about their school work, school exams and being bullied at school. Fewer thought that teachers do a good job and that their school was helping them to prepare for life. A larger proportion of the non-affiliates thought that school was boring (49 per cent) than those from the four religious groups. The research reveals that this was the group which was the least positive about their school and education.

9.3.2 Christianity

Of the four religious groups it was the Christian adolescents who had the smallest proportion who worried about their schoolwork (69 per cent), their exams (77 per cent) and being bullied (34 per cent). Compared with the other three religious group a higher proportion of them thought that school was boring (38 per cent). The Christian adolescents appear to be either more relaxed or more complacent about their education than the teenagers in the other religious groups.

9.3.3 Hinduism

A greater proportion of the Hindu adolescents in Walsall than any other group were happy at school (86 per cent), liked the people they went to school with (94 per cent NS), and were worried about their school work (81 per cent) and their exams (90 per cent). They were the group with the smallest proportion who found school boring (22 per cent). They appear to be the group that is most satisfied and serious about their schooling, and are possibly the keenest on academic achievement.

9.3.4 Islam

A smaller proportion of the Muslims than any other group liked the people they went to school with (88 per cent), although these differences were statistically not significant. In practice many Muslim parents place a great stress on education for their children,[6] although the 2001 national census found that almost a third (31 per cent) of Muslims of working age in Great Britain had no qualifications, which was the highest proportion for any religious group.[7] Caroline Hayden in the *Times Educational Supplement* (22 August 1978) (quoted in Joly, 1995: 121) saw in the young Asians' tendency to opt for an academic rather that vocational orientation 'a reflection of parental values'. These expectations may be why a smaller proportion of the Muslims (70 per cent) than any of the other religious groups thought that their school was helping them to prepare for life. Add to this the fact that a higher proportion of them were worried about being bullied at school (40 per cent) than any other group, and we may have some of the reasons why in parts of the Muslim community there has been such a strong desire to establish Muslim schools.

Traditionally, those from the Indian subcontinent have had a great respect for teachers (Joly, 1995: 122). Many of the Muslim adolescents attend Islamic classes (*madrasas*) after school each day where they experience very different teaching styles, which place emphasis on the authority of the (male) teacher or imam.[8] Thus it is not surprising that a greater proportion of the Muslims (60 per cent) than any other group thought that 'teachers do a good job'.

9.3.5 Sikhism

Generally Sikh parents have high expectations of the educational system and high aspirations for their children (Ballard, 1989: 216).[9] However, compared with the other three religious groups they have the smallest proportion who are happy at their school (70 per cent) and fewer of them thought that teachers do a good job (46 per cent). Despite this, more Sikhs claimed that their school was helping them prepare for life (74 per cent) than any other group.

9.4 Summary

Compared with the White British, more of the South Asian British pupils were positive about their teachers and their school and also thought that it was a good preparation for life. They were more worried about their schoolwork, their exams and about being bullied.

When we examine the influence of religion we find that the non-affiliates were the group who were least happy at school, with fewer of them believing that it was a good preparation for life and more of them finding school boring. They were the most negative about their teachers, and the least worried about school work, exams and being bullied. Compared with the other three religious groups fewer of the adolescent Christians were worried about school work, exams and being bullied and most likely to be bored by school. The Hindu pupils were more worried about their school work and exams than the other groups yet happier about their school and their fellow pupils. The Muslim group had the smallest proportion who thought that school was helping them to prepare for life and the largest proportion who were worried about being bullied. Of the four religious groups the Sikhs were least happy with their school and with their teachers, yet more likely to feel that school was preparing them for life.

10
Work and employment

10.1 Introduction

Patterns of employment have changed over recent decades. Few people today presume that they will work for one employer all their life and most expect to change jobs several times or even retrain for a new career. There is a significant increase in part-time working, flexi-working and cottage industries, where people work from their homes. There has also been an increase in temporary contracts and in buying in skills rather than using in-house resources. Burgess and Rees (1994: 27) found that the mean job tenure for men declined from 10.5 years in 1975 to 9.4 in 1991, and that this was due to a rapid fall in the proportion of men holding jobs for five years or more (down from 62 per cent in 1982 to 54 per cent in 1991). They also observed that those aged eighteen to twenty-five are over-represented in the insecure end of the jobs market (1994: 28).

Francis and Kay put six statements to the adolescents, three about work and three about unemployment (table 10.1). A large majority (94 per cent) thought that hard work was important. Just over three-quarters thought that a job gives a person a sense of purpose and the vast majority of the teenagers were ambitious for promotion when they were in employment (86 per cent). Just under one-fifth (18 per cent) thought that they would prefer to be unemployed and on social security than be in a job they did not like. The majority of the adolescents did not want to be unemployed (86 per cent). Finally, just over half thought that most unemployed people could get a job if they really wanted to (56 per cent).

The same statements were put to the young people in Walsall (table 10.2). The results were broadly similar when compared with the Walsall findings. The proportion of the Walsall adolescents who

Table 10.1 Work: Francis and Kay

	Agree %	Not certain %	Disagree %
I think it is important to work hard when I get a job	94	4	2
A job gives you a sense of purpose	77	19	4
I want to get to the top in my work when I get a job	86	11	3
I would rather be unemployed on social security that get a job I don't like doing	18	24	58
I would not like to be unemployed	86	5	9
Most unemployed people could have a job if they really wanted to	56	24	20

Source: Francis and Kay (1995: 176)

Table 10.2 Work: an overview of Walsall adolescents

	Agree %	Not certain %	Disagree %
I think it is important to work hard when I get a job	95	3	2
A job gives you a sense of purpose	75	21	4
I want to get to the top in my work when I get a job	89	9	2
I would rather be unemployed on social security that get a job I don't like doing	21	25	54
I would not like to be unemployed	83	8	10
Most unemployed people could have a job if they really wanted to	56	24	20

Source: Smith (2002: 204)

thought that it was important to work hard when in employment was only 1 percentage point greater, although a smaller proportion thought that a job gives a sense of purpose (75 per cent compared with 77 per cent). The proportion of teenagers in Walsall who were ambitious to get to the top was 3 percentage points greater. Russell (1998: 92) reported the responses of 604 British workers and found that 23 per cent thought that 'opportunity of advancement' was 'very important'. This was a decline of 3 percentage points since a similar question was put to 750 people in 1989.

When it came to unemployment the proportion of the Walsall adolescents who thought they would rather be unemployed on social security than getting a job they did not like was 3 percentage points greater (21 per cent compared with 18 per cent). Russell (1998: 92) found that 49 per cent of the respondents thought that 'an interesting job' was 'very important', an increase of 1 percentage point since a similar question was asked in a survey in 1989. A smaller proportion were worried about unemployment than in the Francis and Kay cohort (83 per cent compared with 86 per cent).

The responses of both the Walsall group and the Francis and Kay group to the statement 'Most unemployed people could have a job if they really wanted to' were identical (56 per cent). Furnham and Gunter (1989: 164) found relatively similar responses from the adolescents in their study, that is, 52 per cent thought that young people could get work if they looked hard and often enough.

The young people in both groups were overwhelmingly positive about work. They were ambitious and wanted to work hard. Conversely, most of them were negative about being unemployed and realized that they might have to be in a job which they did not like rather than be unemployed.

10.2 The influence of Asian culture on attitudes towards to work

The sample was divided into the White British and the South Asian British groups (table 10.3).

A vast amount of research has been undertaken to examine the levels of employment, unemployment, job aspirations and the type of work being done by people from different ethnic groups, which shows that there are many factors, such as ethnicity, which needs to be taken into account when analysing the data.[1]

Table 10.3 Work: the influence of Asian culture

	White British %	South Asian British %	χ^2	p<
I think it is important to work hard when I get a job	95	97	3	NS
A job gives you a sense of purpose	74	79	6	.05
I want to get to the top in my work when I get a job	88	95	21	.001
I would rather be unemployed on social security that get a job I don't like doing	20	25	6	.05
I would not like to be unemployed	83	82	<1	NS
Most unemployed people could have a job if they really wanted to	54	64	19	.001

Source: Smith (2002: 213)

Even within ethnic minority groups there are significant variations, with Pakistanis and Bangladeshis having the worse-paid jobs and highest levels of unemployment (Rex and Tomlinson, 1979: 108–9; Jones, 1993: 151). Coleman and Hendry (1999: 165) found that those Asians who had come to Britain from east Africa were more likely to have professional jobs.

The situation is further complicated by the different attitudes about the employment of women. A larger proportion of the Asian community were unhappy about women working (Commission for Racial Equality, 1978: 47–8), although some of the women would like to have been in paid employment (Brah and Shaw, 1993: 2–3).

When compared with the White British teenagers the proportion of the South Asian British teenagers in Walsall who thought that a job gave a sense of purpose was 5 percentage points greater and a greater proportion wanted to get to the top in their work (95 per cent compared with 88 per cent). This reflects a large body of research which has shown that Asians have higher educational and vocational aspiration than their white contemporaries.[2] Ballard has suggested that part of the reason for these high aspirations may be that most immigrants have not come from the poorest sections of their society, since such people do not have the financial means to travel to another country. He argued that immigrants mainly come from 'families of middling status' and are basically entrepreneurs (1994a: 9).

This piece of research reveals that the proportion of the Asian teenagers in Walsall who would rather be unemployed than have a job they did not like was 5 percentage points greater when compared with the White British adolescents. Other research has shown consistently that there have been higher levels of unemployment among ethnic minorities than amongst the white population in the UK[3] and this appears to have been the case in Walsall. In 1996 it was reported that the Palfrey Ward had one of the highest percentages of unemployed black and Asian under-twenty-five-year-old men in the country (*Walsall Observer*, 19 January 1996). Other research has also shown that a higher proportion of ethnic minorities were working in semi-skilled and unskilled jobs, in dirtier jobs, and were involved in shift work (Rex and Tomlinson, 1979: 109).

It has also been observed that there is a far higher proportion of Asians, compared with the white population, who are self-employed and who work in retailing. Generally this has required long hours of work and comparatively low levels of pay.[4] These factors may be part of the reason why a higher proportion of the Asian adolescents than the white teenagers are concerned about job satisfaction.

Unemployment has been a serious problem in the United Kingdom for a number of years, both the total numbers of those unemployed and as the average length of unemployment. In the mid-1990s, just before this research was undertaken, Walsall had one of the highest rates in the country of people who have been unemployed for more than a year (*Walsall Observer*, 29 December 1995). Against this background, it is interesting to note that compared with the White British teenagers a greater proportion of the South Asian British teenagers in Walsall thought that unemployed people could get a job if they really wanted to (64 per cent compared with 54 per cent). This may, in part, be due to the enterprise culture of those from an Asian background. Owen, quoting statistics from the 1991 census, showed that there were more self-employed people among the ethnic minorities than whites (20 per cent of men and 8 per cent of women from ethnic minorities, compared with 18 per cent of white men and 7 per cent of white women were self-employed) (Owen, 1996: 23).

10.3 The influence of religion on attitudes towards work

Table 10.4 shows the results when the statistics are broken down into the four religious groups and the non-affiliates.

10.3.1 Non-affiliates

The non-affiliates group (along with the Hindus) had the smallest proportion of those who thought that it was important to work hard when in employment (94 per cent) and the fewest who thought that a job gives a sense of purpose (71 per cent). They were also the group who were the least ambitious, with only 87 per cent wanting to get to the top in their work when they got a job.

Table 10.4 Work: the influence of religion

	Chr %	Hindu %	Muslim %	Sikh %	NA %	χ^2	p<
I think it is important to work hard when I get a job	97	94	96	98	94	19	.001
A job gives you a sense of purpose	78	79	79	79	71	23	.001
I want to get to the top in my work when I get a job	90	96	94	95	87	31	.001
I would rather be unemployed on social security than get a job I don't like doing	20	12	29	25	20	18	.01
I would not like to be unemployed	86	89	77	85	81	24	.001
Most unemployed people could have a job if they really wanted to	52	60	64	66	55	23	.001

Source: Smith (2002: 206)

10.3.2 Christianity

The adolescent Christians were the group with the smallest proportion of respondents who thought that most unemployed people could get a job if they really wanted it (52 per cent).

10.3.3 Hinduism

Of the four religious groups, the Hindu teenagers had the smallest proportion of those who thought it is important to work hard when one has a job (94 per cent, the same as the non-affiliates). Equal with the Muslims and Sikhs, there were 79 per cent who thought that a job gives a person a sense of purpose, which was higher than both the Christian group (78 per cent) and the non-affiliates group (71 per cent). A larger number of the Hindu adolescents appeared to be more ambitious than the other groups, with 96 per cent wanting to get to the top in their work and a smaller proportion who would rather be unemployed than have a job they did not like doing (12 per cent). They also had the largest group who did not want to be unemployed (89 per cent). These statistics give a profile of the Hindu teenagers in which more were ambitious and more were determined to work hard than in the other groups. The data may reflect the entrepreneurial skills of the Hindus who came to Britain from Africa and who have proved to be more successful than Sikhs and Muslims in areas such as retailing (Robinson and Flintoff, 1982: 257–8). Ghuman (1994: 62) observed that Hindus and Sikhs had higher vocational aspirations than Muslim teenagers.[5] Modood et al. (1997: 113–14) found that the mean earnings for male and female Hindus were higher than those of Sikhs, which in turn were higher than those earned by Muslims. There was also a far higher proportion of high earners in the Hindu community than in the Sikh and Muslim communities.[6]

It is the Hindus who came to Britain via east Africa who have been some of the most successful of the ethnic minorities, both academically (Ballard and Vellins, 1985: 261) and commercially, although in the early years they had to take whatever jobs they could find (Warrier, 1994: 197–8). Since then they have become one of the most successful communities from the Indian subcontinent (Knott, 1994: 223; Lyon and West, 1995: 399–419).

10.3.4 Islam

The same proportion of Muslims as of the Hindus and Sikhs thought that it is important to work hard when in employment (79 per cent). They had the highest proportion who would rather be unemployed on social security than get a job they did not like doing (29 per cent) and the lowest proportion who would not like to be unemployed (77 per cent). Part of the reason for this may be that for many years Muslims have tended to work in low paid jobs (Modood et al., 1997: 163; Peach, 2005: 27; Anwar, 2005: 34–6). Anwar (1985: 97) pointed out that the 1971 census revealed that Pakistani males were more likely to be employed in occupations which paid low wages and to work in manual jobs rather than in management. He also observed that the levels of unemployment among Pakistani school-leavers was twice that of the White British (Anwar, 1995: 243). Modood found that many Hindus, Muslims and Sikhs thought that they were discriminated against in the job market because of their race and religion, with Muslims facing more prejudice than the others (Modood et al., 1997: 133–44). Despite this, there is evidence that some parents have high vocational aspirations for their children as do the adolescents themselves (Carey and Shukur, 1985: 410; Joly, 1995: 121).

Another factor which may have influenced the Muslims' responses is the expectation that daughters should stay at home to raise a family. Afshar discovered home working was prevalent in all the households she studied and 'employment was seen by all as secondary to motherhood and child rearing' (Afshar, 1989: 222). Jones (1993: 158) summed up a piece of research by the PSI: 'Bangladeshi and Pakistani women, who are nearly all Muslims, have very low rates of economic activity; very high proportions do not work outside the home.' Joly found that over half (54 per cent) of the Muslim parents in Birmingham did not want their daughters to stay on at school after the age of sixteen and only one in seven thought that their daughters might train for a profession (Joly, 1995: 121). Mizra (1989: 17) noted that Muslim parents often made a distinction between suitable and unsuitable jobs for their daughters. For example: 'Many parents will not allow their daughters to enter nursing because it would mean coming into contact with men, but if she were a doctor, it is accepted because she would be higher up the professional and social scale.' Brah and Shaw found that the Muslim women did not think that they should simply accept any kind of job (1993: 3), which would support the view that only certain types of jobs are culturally acceptable.

Brah (1993: 456) found that Muslim women worked (that is, paid work) less that other Asian and non-Asian women in Britain, yet 'the most striking aspect of the responses we received was that an overwhelming majority of the women we interviewed considered that women should have the right to undertake paid work' (p. 450), and 'Contrary to the stereotype, however, only about a quarter of our respondents gave their families' opposition to women holding jobs away from the home on the grounds of 'izzat' and 'purdah' as the major reason why they were not doing paid work' (p. 452).

10.3.5 Sikhism

The Sikh adolescents had the highest proportion of those who thought it is important to work hard when in employment (98 per cent), that a job gives a sense of purpose (79 per cent, joint equal with the Hindus and Muslims) and the largest proportion who thought that most unemployed people could have a job if they really wanted one (66 per cent).

Singh (1992: 46), summarizing some other pieces of research, concluded that British Sikh men were significantly under-represented in professional, employer and other non-manual categories and over-represented in skilled and semi-skilled manual categories. He also pointed out that 'Within the Sikh community in Bradford there was a clear polarisation of jobs, that is, either the Sikhs were concentrated in lower level jobs or on the other extreme, in socially and economically higher-status jobs' (p. 48). Bhachu (1985: abstract in the front of the book) noted:

> the competitive nature of the egalitarian Punjabi society strongly influences the strategies parents adopt to educate their children and to motivate them to succeed in the educational system. These values are applicable in Britain despite migration from urban areas and also despite the varying caste and class positions of the parents. [and] The Punjabi attitude towards education is purpose-orientated . . . Education has to be instrumental in getting an individual a suitable job . . . (p. 5).

Dosanjh (n.d.: 14) found that 'There is a very strong desire among the Punjabi parents for upward mobility in their children'. The vast majority of the parents expected their children to have better jobs than themselves because they had a better education. Singh (1992: 48) surveyed Sikh women in Bradford and discovered that '55% of the wives of the heads of households were in full-time employment'. They were mainly employed in the textile industry in unskilled and semi-skilled work.

These observations on the work of Sikh men and women are in line with the findings from the Walsall adolescent Sikhs, who thought it was important to work hard, that work gives a person a sense of purpose and that most unemployed people could find a job if they really wanted one.

10.4 Summary

When the influence of ethnicity is examined it reveals a picture in which more of the South Asian British teenagers thought that a job gives a sense of purpose, in which more were ambitious to get to the top and more of whom thought that most unemployed people could get a job if they really wanted to. However, a higher proportion indicated that they would also rather be unemployed than be in a job they did not like.

Turning to the influence of religion we can see from the responses of the non-affiliates that they are the group who are least motivated, the least ambitious and the group who are most sceptical that work can provide a sense of purpose. Religion would appear to stimulate motivation and expand horizons. Of the three religious groups, the Christians were slightly less optimistic that employment can give a sense of purpose, they were the least ambitious and a smaller proportion of them thought that the unemployed could find work if they really wanted it. The Hindus were the most ambitious, with the greatest proportion who did not want to be unemployed and who were willing to take jobs that they might not like. The Muslims were the group that was less worried about being unemployed especially if they could not find a job that they liked. The Sikhs had the highest proportion that thought that the unemployed could find jobs if they were determined.

11
Global and national concerns

11.1 Introduction

The media often portray young people as being hedonistic, but there is plenty of evidence that they can be altruistic. For example, since 1979 the annual BBC's Children in Need appeal and since 1984 Live Aid have both been supported by millions of young people in schools, colleges and youth organizations, such as church youth groups, and the Scouts and Guides. Their energy has been expressed in other ways as well, such as in the lead-up to the Iraq War when on 15 February 2003 large numbers of young people were among the one million people who demonstrated on the streets of London. Negative caricatures of young people in Britain today need to be challenged. But what are the issues which young people are concerned about today? Six statements were put to the adolescents about national and global issues (table 11.1).

Responses showed that 63 per cent of the teenagers were concerned about the risk of nuclear war and three-fifths were worried about Third World poverty. An even larger proportion were worried about the risk of polluting the environment (66 per cent), whilst only 18 per cent thought there was too much television violence. Nearly one-third (31 per cent) argued that pornography was too readily available. One quarter thought that there was nothing they could do to help solve the world's problems.

Shortly before the research on the Walsall adolescents took place, the war in the Baltic states broke out. It provoked a public debate in the local media,[1] out of which a number of initiatives arose, including the sending of several aid convoys. During the mid-1990s these convoys had a very high profile in the local newspapers.[2] The war also produced a number of human interest stories from the conflict, showing a concern for the problems in eastern Europe.[3]

Table 11.1 Global and national concerns: Francis and Kay

	Agree %	Not certain %	Disagree %
I am concerned about the risk of nuclear war	63	22	15
I am concerned about the poverty of the Third World	60	27	13
I am concerned about the risk of pollution to the environment	66	25	9
There is too much violence on television	18	22	60
Pornography is too readily available	31	36	33
There is nothing I can do to help solve the world's problems	25	31	44

Source: Francis and Kay (1995: 70)

One might have presumed that the wide publicity given to the conflict might have influenced the responses of the Walsall teenagers, who were asked to respond to the same statements as those in the Frances and Kay study, with an additional statement about the National Lottery. Their responses are shown in table 11.2. However, compared with the study by Francis and Kay (1995), a smaller proportion of the adolescents in Walsall were concerned about the global issues of nuclear war (44 per cent compared with 63 per cent), the poverty of the Third World (53 per cent compared with 60 per cent) and pollution (59 per cent compared with 66 per cent).

The proportion of the Walsall adolescents who expressed a concern that there was too much violence on the television was 4 percentage points greater. More of the Walsall teenagers thought that pornography was too readily available (40 per cent compared with 31 per cent). A higher proportion thought that they there was nothing they could do to solve the world's problems (29 per cent compared with 25 per cent). Just over half (57 per cent) thought that the National Lottery was a good thing.

Compared with the adolescents in the Francis and Kay cohort, a higher proportion of teenagers in Walsall were uncertain what they felt about the global issues and in each case a smaller proportion expressed concern. At the same time, a larger proportion

Table 11.2 Global and national concerns: an overview

	Agree %	Not certain %	Disagree %
I am concerned about the risk of nuclear war	44	33	23
I am concerned about the poverty of the Third World	53	30	17
I am concerned about the risk of pollution to the environment	59	28	13
There is too much violence on television	23	22	56
Pornography is too readily available	40	34	26
I think the National Lottery is a good thing	57	21	23
There is nothing I can do to help solve the world's problems	29	30	41

Source: Smith (2002: 218)

thought that there was nothing they could do to change the global situation. Conversely, more of the teenagers in Walsall expressed concern about television violence and pornography. It would appear that the Walsall adolescents were more parochial in their concerns.

11.2 The influence of Asian culture

The sample was divided into the White British and the South Asian British (table 11.3). There are significant statistical differences in the responses to all the statements of at least $p<.05$,[4] except in response to 'I am concerned about the risk of nuclear war' and 'There is nothing I can do to help solve the world's problems'.

In response to each of the statements more of the South Asian British adolescents expressed concern. The proportion who were worried about Third World poverty was 12 percentage points greater, perhaps because, as already suggested, many of them had families in the Third World or had visited families in those parts of the world. They were also more concerned about the risk of pollution (64 per cent compared with 58 per cent), about television violence (33 per cent compared with 21 per cent) and the availability of pornography (45 per cent compared with 39 per cent).

Table 11.3 Global and national concerns: the influence of Asian culture

	White British %	South Asian British %	χ^2	p<
I am concerned about the risk of nuclear war	44	47	2	NS
I am concerned about the poverty of the Third World	51	63	26	.001
I am concerned about the risk of pollution to the environment	58	64	6	.05
There is too much violence on television	21	33	40	.001
Pornography is too readily available	39	45	5	.05
I think that National Lottery is a good thing	59	43	46	.001
There is nothing I can do to help solve the world's problems	29	28	1	NS

Source: Smith (2002: 225)

The proportion of the South Asian British teenagers who thought that the National Lottery was a good thing was 16 percentage points smaller.

11.3 The influence of religion

The teenagers were divided into the four main religious groups and the non-affiliates, and the results are set out in table 11.4.

11.3.1 Non-affiliates

The non-affiliates were the least concerned about the risk of nuclear war (39 per cent), the poverty of the Third World (45 per cent), and the risk of pollution to the environment (53 per cent). Fewer of them thought that there was too much violence on television (17 per cent) and that pornography was too readily available (37 per cent). A larger proportion of them thought that there was nothing they could do to help solve the world's problems (32 per cent) and that the National Lottery was a good thing (63 per cent).

Table 11.4 Global and national concerns: by religion

	Chr %	Hindu %	Muslim %	Sikh %	NA %	χ^2	p<
I am concerned about the risk of nuclear war	50	40	47	48	39	37	.001
I am concerned about the poverty of the Third World	60	68	62	62	45	96	.001
I am concerned about the risk of pollution to the environment	65	62	64	64	53	49	.001
There is too much violence on television	25	31	43	21	17	97	.001
Pornography is too readily available	44	40	47	44	37	20	.001
I think that National Lottery is a good thing	53	50	28	61	63	128	.001
There is nothing I can do to help solve the world's problems	26	22	30	26	32	12	.05

Source: Smith (2002: 222)

11.3.2 Christianity

Of all the groups, the Christian adolescents had the highest proportion who were concerned about the risk of nuclear war (50 per cent) and the risk of pollution to the environment (65 per cent). By contrast, of the four religious groups, the Christians had the smallest proportion who were concerned about the poverty of the Third World (60 per cent).

11.3.3 Hinduism

Compared with the three other religious groups, the Hindu adolescents had quite a distinct profile. A smaller proportion of them were concerned about the risk of nuclear war (40 per cent) and the risk of pollution to the environment (62 per cent). More were concerned about the poverty of the Third World (68 per cent). A smaller proportion of them thought that there was nothing they could do to solve the world's problems (22 per cent) and that pornography was too readily available (0 per cent).

11.3.4 Islam

A larger proportion of the adolescent Muslims, compared with the other groups thought that there was too much violence of television (43 per cent) and that pornography was too readily available (47 per cent). Although some members of the Muslim community in Walsall had been concerned about issues such as the environment and toxic waste,[5] nevertheless, compared with the other religious groups, more of the Muslims thought that there was nothing they could do to help solve the world's problems (30 per cent), reflecting a more fatalistic outlook. Only 28 per cent thought that the National Lottery was a good thing, which is a much smaller percentage than any other group. The Muslim adolescents revealed strong feelings concerning personal morality but were not so concerned about global issues.

11.3.5 Sikhism

Of the four religious groups, the Sikh teenagers had the smallest proportion who thought there was too much television violence. This may be because the Sikh tradition has taught that violence is permissible in certain circumstances. Although Guru Nanak, the founder of Sikhism, had little to say on the matter of war and pacifism, his followers accept that they may have to bear arms and in consequence the wearing of a dagger (*kirpan*) is one of the five distinguishing symbols of a Sikh. This group also had the largest proportion who thought that the National Lottery was a good thing (61 per cent).

11.4 Summary

When looking at the influence of ethnicity, we can see that the South Asian British youngsters were more concerned than the White British teenagers about all of the subjects explored. When the criteria of religion was applied to the data, the non-affiliates showed the most distinctive profile with the lowest levels of concerns in all areas and the largest proportion who thought that there was nothing they could do to change the situation. The White British teenagers were more worried about nuclear war and the environment, whilst the South Asian British were more concerned about poverty in the Third World. More of the Muslims were worried about personal morality, such as television violence and pornography, rather than global issues and, of the four religious groups, they had the largest proportion who thought that there was nothing they could do make any difference in solving the world's problems.

12
Young people and politics

12.1 Introduction

When compared with adults, teenagers are less likely to be interested in politics or to be attached to a political party (Park, 1995: 54). Wilkinson and Mulgan summed up their findings: 'The overwhelming story emerging from our research, both quantitatively and qualitative, is of an historic political disconnection. In effect, an entire generation has opted out of party politics' (Wilkinson and Mulgan, 1995: 99). A number of commentators noted the irony that more people voted in the television show *Big Brother* than in the June 2001 British general election. The government has been concerned about the lack of engagement of young people in the political process and has been experimenting with alternative methods of voting, such as by postal ballots and on the Internet. Curtice and Jowell (1997: 91) found that between 1973 and 1996 there was a growing proportion of people in Britain who thought that the system of governing the country could be improved (from 49 per cent to 63 per cent) and between 1974 and 1996 there was a decline in the proportion who thought that any political party would put the needs of the nation above their own interests. There was an increasing level of scepticism about whether politicians were more interested in people's votes than their opinions (growing from 19 per cent in 1974 to 28 per cent in 1996) and a sense that, once elected, politicians quickly lose touch with the people they represent (increasing from 19 per cent in 1974 to 26 per cent in 1996) (Curtice and Jowell, 1997: 93). They also found (pp. 94–5) that between 1985 and 1996 a larger proportion of the population were tolerant of undemocratic protest. Between 1983 and 1996 there was a decline of 12 percentage points in those who thought that 'People should obey the law without exception' (from 53 per cent to 41 per cent) and an increase of 9 percentage points in those who thought that 'On exceptional occasions people should follow their consciences even if it means breaking the law' (from 46 per cent to 55 per cent).

In order to listen to young people's views on politics, Francis and Kay put a number of statements to them (table 12.1). Whilst 17 per cent trusted the Conservative Party, 19 per cent expressed confidence in the Labour Party. Despite this, 49 per cent thought that it made a real difference which party was in power. Some 17 per cent agreed that private medicine should be abolished and one-quarter thought that private schools should be abolished. Only 17 per cent thought that state ownership of industry was a good thing and 18 per cent were satisfied with the local council. Just under one-quarter thought that trade unions have too much power (24 per cent). About one-third of the adolescents thought that immigration into Britain should be restricted (32 per cent).

The same statements were put to the young people in Walsall (table 12.2). Compared with the Francis and Kay sample, the proportion of the Walsall adolescents who had confidence in the Conservative Party was 6 percentage points smaller, while the

Table 12.1 Politics: Francis and Kay

	Agree %	Not certain %	Disagree %
I have confidence in the Conservative Party	17	34	49
I have confidence in the Labour Party	19	36	45
It makes no difference which political party is in power	19	32	49
Private medicine should be abolished	17	42	41
Private schools should be abolished	25	32	42
State ownership of industry is a good thing	17	70	13
The local council does a good job	18	45	37
Trade unions have too much power	24	65	11
I think that immigration into Britain should be restricted	32	38	30

Source: Francis and Kay (1995: 203)

Table 12.2 Politics: an overview of Walsall adolescents

	Agree %	Not certain %	Disagree %
I have confidence in the Conservative Party	11	39	51
I have confidence in the Labour Party	24	42	34
It makes no difference which political party is in power	29	37	34
Private medicine should be abolished	14	45	41
Private schools should be abolished	25	34	42
State ownership of industry is a good thing	16	72	13
The local council does a good job	15	42	43
Trade unions have too much power	24	64	12
I think that immigration into Britain should be restricted	35	38	27

Source: Smith (2002: 226)

proportion who trusted the Labour Party was 5 percentage points greater. Park (1995: 52) found that 51 per cent of the twelve- to nineteen-year-olds identified with the Labour Party, 20 per cent with the Conservatives, 14 per cent with the Liberal Democrats and 14 per cent with other parties. Whilst the question they posed was slightly different, it is interesting that more than twice the proportion of the Walsall adolescents were positive about the Labour Party when compared with the Conservatives (24 per cent compared with 11 per cent), which is not a dissimilar ratio to the responses of the adolescents questioned by Park.

The teenagers were asked if they thought that it made a difference which political party was in office. The proportion of the Walsall adolescents who were sceptical was 10 percentage points greater than those in the Francis and Kay cohort. Other research echoes similar levels of cynicism (Gaskin, Vlaeminke and Fenton, 1996: 14, 19; Curtice and Jowell, 1997: 106), which is also shown in the decline in youth membership of the main political parties in recent years (Wilkinson and Mulgan, 1995: 98–101), a trend which has been going on for some time (Park, 2004: 24–33). Despite this, there is evidence that those adolescents who do join a political party are more likely to be committed to political principles than older members and they are less likely to support a strategy of 'capturing the middle ground' (Seyd, Whiteley and Parry, 1996: 6).

The responses of the Walsall adolescents to the statements about private medicine, education and privatization produced some surprising results. A smaller proportion than in the Francis and Kay group thought that private medicine should be abolished (14 per cent compared with 17 per cent). Both groups had virtually identical views on the abolition of private schooling (25 per cent in favour). The proportion of the Walsall teenagers who thought that state ownership of industry is a good thing was 1 percentage point smaller. Only 15 per cent compared with 18 per cent thought that the council were doing a good job. The views of the two groups on the trade unions was broadly similar with 24 per cent in both groups agreeing that they had too much power. The proportion of the Walsall teenagers who thought that immigration into Britain should be restricted was 3 percentage points greater.

The responses paint a picture of the Walsall teenagers as being generally less certain about their views in this area than the larger sample of Francis and Kay. They are generally further to the left in their political views. A slightly smaller proportion were against the private sector but a larger proportion wished to limit immigration.

12.2 The influence of Asian culture

The responses of the White British and the South Asian British are set out in table 12.3. The responses of the teenage Asians may be influenced, at least in part, by the fact that Asians have been involved in British politics for a relatively short time.[1]

Nearly twice as many of the South Asian British adolescents had confidence in the Labour Party than the White British teenagers (41 per cent compared with 21 per cent), whilst a smaller proportion of them thought that it makes no difference which political party is in power (25 per cent compared with 30 per cent), suggesting that they were slightly less cynical about the political process than the white teenagers. Whilst there is no doubt that some young Asians are very actively involved in politics (Brah, 1996: 43–7), scholars are divided on whether there are significant differences between South Asian British teenagers and white adolescents (Husband, 1994: 94). Sharma (1980: 246) did not find that there were any 'significant differences among Asian and English

Table 12.3 Politics: the influence of Asian culture

	White British %	South Asian British %	χ^2	p<
I have confidence in the Conservative Party	11	10	<1	NS
I have confidence in the Labour Party	21	41	103	.001
It makes no difference which political party is in power	30	25	5	.05
Private medicine should be abolished	13	18	9	.01
Private schools should be abolished	26	19	12	.001
State ownership of industry is a good thing	15	22	19	.001
The local council does a good job	13	26	58	.001
Trade unions have too much power	24	23	<1	NS
I think that immigration into Britain should be restricted	39	17	89	.001

Source: Smith (2002: 235)

[sic] adolescents' perceptions of the importance of the institutions such as trades unions, general elections, taxation and courts of law'.

In general, the levels of registration to vote among South Asian British have been lower than among White British.[2] Despite this, research shows that, for those who have registered, a higher proportion of Asian actually voted (Anwar, 1994b: 24ff). The greater level of confidence in the Labour Party may partly be due to the larger number of Asian Labour candidates who have stood for election[3] and the fact that over the past thirty years the majority of Asians have voted Labour.[4]

The responses to the statements on private services and privatization were confusing. More of the Asian adolescents (by 5 percentage points) thought that private medicine should be abolished fewer (by 7 percentage points) thought that private school should be abolished and a higher proportion thought that state ownership of industry is a good thing (22 per cent compared with 15 per cent). The proportion of the Asian adolescents who thought that the council were going a good job was 13 percentage points greater but a much smaller proportion of them thought that immigration into Britain should be restricted (17 per cent compared with 39 per cent).

12.3 The influence of religion

The sample was divided into the four religious groups and the non-affiliates and the responses are set out in table 12.4.

12.3.1 Non-affiliates

Compared with the four religious groups, the non-affiliates had the lowest proportion who had confidence in the Labour Party (19 per cent), the lowest proportion who thought that private medicine should be abolished (13 per cent), the highest proportion who believed that private schools should be abolished (26 per cent, which was the same as the Christian group), the lowest proportion who were happy with the local council (12 per cent) and the highest proportion who thought that immigration into Britain should be restricted (39 per cent, the same proportion as the Christian group).

Table 12.4 Politics: the influence of religion in Walsall

	Chr %	Hindu %	Muslim %	Sikh %	NA %	χ^2	$p<$
I have confidence in the Conservative Party	12	8	15	4	10	17	.01
I have confidence in the Labour Party	23	32	48	35	19	125	.001
It makes no difference which political party is in power	31	28	26	24	29	6	NS
Private medicine should be abolished	14	17	21	16	13	12	.05
Private schools should be abolished	26	17	19	19	26	12	.05
State ownership of industry is a good thing	14	10	25	23	15	30	.001
The local council does a good job	14	21	34	17	12	88	.001
Trade unions have too much power	22	20	27	21	25	7	NS
I think that immigration into Britain should be restricted	39	10	19	18	39	91	.001

Source: Smith (2002: 230)

12.3.2 Christianity

The adolescent Christians in Walsall were the group with the highest proportion who thought that it makes no difference which political party is in power (31 per cent NS). As described above, equal with the non-affiliates, they had the highest proportion who thought that private schools should be abolished (26 per cent) and that immigration should be restricted (39 per cent). Compared with the other three religious groups they had the lowest proportion who thought that private medicine should be abolished (14 per cent).

12.3.3 Hinduism

The Hindu teenagers had the lowest proportion who thought that private schools should be abolished (17 per cent), which may reflect the high level of academic aspiration and achievement of the Hindu community in Britain. They also had the lowest proportion who considered that state ownership of industry is a good thing (10 per cent), that trade unions have too much power (20 per cent NS) and that immigration into Britain should be restricted (10 per cent).

12.3.4 Islam

Compared with the other groups, more of the Muslims had confidence in the Conservative Party (15 per cent) and in the Labour Party (48 per cent). In other words, a far higher proportion of the Muslims compared with the other groups had strong political views and had trust in the political system. This may be partly because a Muslim, at least in theory, makes no separation between the world of politics and the world of religion, and therefore places a high value on politics as a way of governing society. As Sarwar (1982: 177) put it, 'Religion and politics are one and the same in Islam'. Having said this, some parts of the Muslim community, such as the Barelvis, are less interested and involved in politics (King, 1994: 3).

In the earliest phases of immigration much time and energy was taken up with employment issues, visas and maintaining links with their home countries. As the community became more settled, and many Muslims realized they would not be returning to their country of origin to live, so involvement both in local and national politics began to grow. In general elections Muslims have tended to vote Labour (Joly, 1995: 11, 81, 90–4), although there are plenty of exceptions to this[5] and there is no uniformity across the Asian community (Werbner, 1990: 81). In local elections there appears to be an even greater diversity of voting patterns (Eade: 1992: 34). Indeed, there is some evidence that their support for the Labour Party has been declining (Wahhab, 1989: 12) and as time has gone on so the political allegiance of the Muslim community has become more diversified.

With the increase in the Muslim population in Britain in recent years, some leaders have argued that they should try to influence the major political parties and highlight their own agenda and priorities. An example of this is the Muslim charter of 1984 that suggested that Muslims should vote for the candidate who would support Muslim issues, especially in schools (Joly, 1995: 92). Murad (1986: 9) also believed that politics was the way to change the educational system and to spread Islam. Joly (1995: 88) pointed out that, as well as national politics, many Muslims have been involved in 'non-electoral politics' and in particular she identified four areas: anti-racist campaign groups, anti-deportation campaigns, divided family campaigns and campaigns against police violence and against the sentencing of immigrants for 'political' crimes.

Traditionally, the leadership of the Muslim community has come from its religious leaders. However, many of the younger generation have been critical of them and in some areas alternative secular leadership has emerged.[6] This has sometimes caused tension between the religious and the secular agendas (Eade, 1992: 41).

Compared with the other groups, the Muslim adolescents had higher proportions who thought that private medicine should be abolished (21 per cent), that state ownership of industry is a good thing (25 per cent), that the local council does a good job (34 per cent) and that trade unions have too much power (27 per cent NS).

12.3.5 Sikhism

Of all the groups, the Sikh adolescents in Walsall had the smallest proportion who had confidence in the Conservative Party (4 per cent) and, after the Muslims (48 per cent), the second highest proportion who had confidence in the Labour Party (35 per cent). It might be argued that they appear to be the most left wing of the four religious groups, since the Muslims have a larger proportion who had confidence in the Conservative Party. However, the Sikhs were also the least cynical about the difference that political parties can make, with only 24 per cent (NS) believing that it made no difference which political party was in power.

In general, Sikhs have tended to have a high level of involvement in politics at all levels, including local politics (Ghuman, 1980: 313–14), the Indian Workers' Association (Tatla, 1993a: 96), Punjabi politics [7] and British party politics, where they have tended to vote Labour (Singh, 1992: 30). The first Sikh to be elected to the House of Commons was in 1992, and in the following election in 1997 two Sikhs were elected (Tatla, 1999: 100). The Sikh community has had success in campaigning over a number of issues and in particular the right to wear the turban.[8] Like young Muslims, there is clear evidence that some of the younger Sikhs have developed a greater political awareness and involvement.[9]

12.4 Summary

When we examine the effect of ethnicity on the political views of the young people we find that the South Asian British were less likely to be cynical about politics. They were more likely to support the Labour Party, state ownership of industry and their local council. A much higher proportion were against limiting immigration.

Turning to the influence of religion, the non-affiliates had the smallest proportion of Labour Party supporters and the smallest proportion who wanted to abolish private medicine. Yet they had the highest proportion (along with the Christians) who wanted to abolish private schools. They were the most cynical about the effectiveness of the local council. The Hindus had the smallest proportions who wanted to abolish private schools, who thought that state ownership of industry was positive and who wanted immigration to be restricted. They appear to be the most liberal of all the groups. The Muslims had the highest levels of support for political parties, both Conservative and Labour. They were the group that was most positive about state ownership of industry and the effectiveness of the local council. More of them than any other group wished to abolish private medicine. The Sikhs had the lowest level of support for the Conservative Party and the smallest proportion (equal with the Muslims) who wanted private schools to be abolished.

13
Religious beliefs in the contemporary world

13.1 Introduction

In chapter 2 I examined religious practice among teenagers and found that 77 per cent chose to use religious categories in their description of themselves and fewer than a quarter (23 per cent) claimed to be non-religious or did not wish to state their religion. Additionally, 51 per cent had attended worship in a church in the previous year and a quarter of them claimed to pray regularly. But to what extent do these practices translate into religious beliefs? In order to explore this, twelve statements were put to the Walsall teenagers. Four of the statements were general and applicable to all the teenagers ('I believe in God', 'I believe God punishes people', 'I believe in life after death' and 'I believe God made the world'). The last statement was subtly different from the one used in the Francis and Kay study which had added the specifically Judeo-Christian rider 'in six days and rested on the seventh'. It was decided to omit this phrase since it might be misunderstood by the young people and the responses of those who practised non-Christian religions would be difficult to interpret. However, two specifically Christian statements of belief ('I believe that Jesus Christ is the Son of God' and 'I believe that Jesus Christ really rose from the dead') were retained, but two extra statements (about reincarnation and Mohammed) were added: 'I believe that Mohammed is the Prophet of the one God'. Finally, it was decided to find out what proportion of the adolescents held an exclusivist position with regard to their own or to another religion. Therefore four new statements were added: 'I believe that Christianity/Hinduism/Islam/Sikhism is the only true religion.'

In order to set the scene we turn first to the responses of the teenagers to the Francis and Kay research (table 13.1): 39 per cent

112 *Growing Up in Multi-Faith Britain*

Table 13.1 Religious beliefs: Francis and Kay

	Agree %	Not certain %	Disagree %
I believe in God	39	35	26
I believe God punishes people who do wrong	19	39	42
I believe in life after death	41	41	18
I believe that God made the world in six days and rested on the seventh	17	42	41
I believe that Jesus Christ is the Son of God	47	34	19
I believe that Jesus Christ really rose from the dead	30	43	27
I think Christianity is the only true religion	16	42	42

Source: Francis and Kay (1995: 137)

believed in God;[1] 19 per cent of the young people thought that God punishes people who do wrong; and just over 40 per cent believed in life after death. In response to the statement 'I believe that God made the world', 17 per cent agreed, 47 per cent thought that Jesus is the Son of God, and 30 per cent believed in the resurrection. Some 16 per cent agreed with the statement that 'Christianity is the only true religion'. We now compare these responses to those of the Walsall teenagers (table 13.2).

The proportion of the Walsall adolescents who believed in God was 7 percentage points greater (46 per cent compared with 39 per cent). Just under one third of the teenagers (30 per cent) believed that God punishes people compared with 19 per cent of the Francis and Kay cohort. In response to the statement about life after death, 51 per cent of the Walsall teenagers agreed compared with 41 per cent. These figures are higher than those found in some other studies.[2] The responses to the statement on creation produced starkly different levels of responses but they were not comparing like with like, as noted above (37 per cent agreed compared with 17 per cent). The responses of the two groups to the statement on the resurrection of Jesus Christ produced broadly similar responses, with 28 per cent of the Walsall adolescents agreeing compared with 30 per cent. When comparing the exclusivist claims about

Table 13.2 Religious beliefs: an overview of Walsall adolescents

	Agree %	Not certain %	Disagree %
I believe in God	46	28	26
I believe God punishes people who do wrong	30	33	37
I believe in life after death	51	33	16
I believe that God made the world	37	35	28
I believe that Jesus Christ is the Son of God	45	31	25
I believe that Jesus really rose from the dead	28	41	31
I believe in reincarnation	30	41	29
I believe that Mohammed is the Prophet of the one God	14	42	44
I think Christianity is the only true religion	20	28	52
I think Hinduism is the only true religion	3	20	77
I think Islam is the only true religion	9	20	72
I think Sikhism is the only true religion	4	21	74

Source: Smith (2002: 88)

Christianity ('I believe that Christianity is the only true religion') we find that a larger proportion of the Walsall adolescents agreed (20 per cent compared with 16 per cent).

Fewer than one-third of the Walsall teenagers believed in reincarnation (30 per cent).[3] 'I believe that Mohammed is the Prophet of the one God' found agreement from 14 per cent of the teenagers. The responses to these last two statements illustrate the way in which religious beliefs from one religion are sometimes held by adherents from other religions or no religion. Thus reincarnation is traditionally a Hindu belief and yet some non-Hindus claim to believe in it. Also, the statement about Mohammed being the Prophet of the one God found agreement with more than those who claimed to be Muslims.

One-fifth thought that Christianity was the only true religion. As would be expected a much smaller proportion (3 per cent) agreed with the proposition 'I believe that Hinduism is the only true religion', although only 2 per cent of the sample claimed that they were Hindus. Although 8 per cent of the adolescents were Muslims, 9 per cent of the sample thought that Islam is the only true religion. The responses to the statement on Sikhism as the only true religion received a broadly similar response, with 4 per cent agreeing. However, in the initial section of the questionnaire 6 per cent said they were Sikhs. It would appear that a smaller proportion of the Sikh teenagers were willing to make exclusivist claims about the truth of their own religion than their Hindu and Muslim counterparts.

13.2 The influence of Asian culture on religious belief

The group of Walsall teenagers was divided between the White British and the South Asian British (table 13.3).

Turning to the first group of four questions we find that in each case a higher proportion of the South Asian adolescents were in agreement with the statements. For example, 84 per cent of the group believed in God whereas only 39 per cent of the White British group believed.[4] Over two-thirds (70 per cent) believed that God

Table 13.3 Religious beliefs: the influence of Asian culture

	White British %	South Asian British %	χ^2	p<
I believe in God	39	84	362	.001
I believe God punishes people who do wrong	22	70	475	.001
I believe in life after death	48	68	71	.001
I believe that God made the world	31	70	293	.001
I believe that Jesus Christ is the Son of God	48	26	86	.001
I believe that Jesus really rose from the dead	30	21	17	.001
I believe in reincarnation	30	33	2	NS
I believe that Mohammed is the Prophet of the one God	7	55	863	.001
I think Christianity is the only true religion	23	3	109	.001
I think Hinduism is the only true religion	2	6	19	.001
I think Islam is the only true religion	3	39	753	.001
I think Sikhism is the only true religion	2	16	191	.001

Source: Smith (2002: 95)

Religious beliefs 115

punishes people who do wrong compared with 22 per cent. The proportion of the Asian adolescents who believed in life after death was 68 per cent (compared with 48 per cent of White British group) and the proportion who believed that God made the world was 70 per cent compared with 31 per cent.

The responses to the two statements about Jesus Christ show that a smaller proportion of the South Asian British agreed with the statements. Just over one quarter (26 per cent) believed that Jesus Christ is the Son of God, compared with 48 per cent of White British group, and 21 per cent believed that Jesus rose from the dead, compared with 30 per cent. The levels of response to the statement 'I believe in incarnation' were fairly similar, although they were not statistically significant. A much higher proportion of the Asian teenagers thought that Mohammed is the Prophet of the one God (55 per cent compared with 7 per cent).

Relatively small proportions of the adolescents held exclusivist views about religion. What was surprising was those who identified themselves with one religion and yet indicated that they believed that another religion was the only true one. Nearly one quarter (23 per cent) of the White British adolescents thought that Christianity is the only true religion, compared with 3 per cent of the South Asian British group. Only 2 per cent of the white group thought that Hinduism was the only true religion, compared with 6 per cent of the Asian adolescents; and only 3 per cent of them thought that Islam was the only true religion, compared with 39 per cent of the Asian group. Finally, 2 per cent of the white teenagers agreed that Sikhism was the only true religion, compared with 16 per cent of the South Asian British adolescents.[5]

13.3 The influence of religion on the different religions

When the group of Walsall teenagers were divided into the four main religious groups and the non-affiliates, a more complex picture emerged (table 13.4.).

13.3.1 Non-affiliates
It is interesting to examine the beliefs of the non-affiliates. Although they were not regularly practising any religion, 24 per cent believed in God and 16 per cent thought that God punishes those who do

116 Growing Up in Multi-Faith Britain

Table 13.4 Religious beliefs: by religion

	Chr %	Hindu %	Muslim %	Sikh %	NA %	χ^2	p<
I believe in God	64	83	91	75	23	832	.001
I believe God punishes people who do wrong	32	54	83	58	16	600	.001
I believe in life after death	58	71	73	60	41	160	.001
I believe that God made the world	50	45	88	57	19	653	.001
I believe that Jesus Christ is the Son of God	73	42	13	38	32	577	.001
I believe that Jesus really rose from the dead	52	22	20	21	15	471	.001
I believe in reincarnation	33	63	11	50	28	128	.001
I believe that Mohammed is the Prophet of the one God	8	14	98	14	6	1622	.001
I think Christianity is the only true religion	36	0	2	6	14	314	.001
I think Hinduism is the only true religion	2	29	1	2	3	201	.001
I think Islam is the only true religion	2	1	79	1	3	1774	.001
I think Sikhism is the only true religion	1	3	1	40	3	635	.001

Source: Smith (2002: 92)

wrong. Nearly one third believed that Christ is the Son of God (32 per cent) and 15 per cent believed that Jesus rose from the dead. Just over two-fifths believed in life after death and 28 per cent believed in reincarnation. About one-fifth believed that God made the world (19 per cent). Some of the non-affiliates expressed exclusivist views of the various religions: 14 per cent for Christianity and 3 per cent each for Hinduism, Islam and Sikhism. A small proportion believed that Mohammed is the Prophet of the one God (6 per cent). This shows that there are significant levels of belief to be found among many of those who do not consider themselves attached to a particular religion.

13.3.2 Christianity

Of the four religious groups the Christians had the smallest proportion who believed in God (64 per cent), that God punishes people who do wrong (32 per cent), in life after death (58 per cent), that Mohammed is the Prophet of the one God (8 per cent) and, equal with the Muslim adolescents, that Sikhism is the only true religion (1 per cent). In contrast, the Christian adolescents had the largest proportion who believed that Jesus Christ is the Son of God (73 per cent), that he rose from the dead (52 per cent) and that Christianity is the only true religion (36 per cent).

13.3.3 Hinduism

Compared with the other three religious groups the Hindu adolescents had the smallest proportion who believed that God made the world (45 per cent), that Christianity is the only true religion (0 per cent) and, equal with the Sikhs, that Islam is the only true religion (1 per cent). They had the largest proportions (63 per cent) who believed in reincarnation and believed that Hinduism is the only true religion (29 per cent).

13.3.4 Islam

Of all the groups, the Muslims had the highest proportions who believed in God (91 per cent), that God punishes people who do wrong (83 per cent), in life after death (73 per cent) and that God made the world 88 per cent). These are all fundamental Islamic tenets of faith. For example, *akhirah* (life after death) is a basic belief for Muslims. Hewitt (1993: 2) and Knott (1992: 39) found that it was widely held by the adolescent Muslim girls in West Yorkshire, although some of them were not afraid to question it. The teenage Muslims also had the highest proportions of those who believed that Mohammed is the Prophet of the one God (98 per cent) and that Islam is the only true religion (79 per cent). They had the smallest proportions who believed that Jesus Christ is the Son of God (13 per cent), in reincarnation (11 per cent), that Hinduism is the only true religion (1 per cent) and, equal with Christianity, that Sikhism is the only true religion (1 per cent). Compared with the other three religious groups it had the smallest proportion who believed that Jesus Christ rose from the dead (20 per cent).

13.3.5 Sikhism

The profile of the adolescent Sikhs in this section is most similar to the profile of the Hindus. Three-quarters claimed belief in God, 58 per cent thought that God punishes those who do wrong and three-fifths agreed with the statement 'I believe in life after death'. Some 57 per cent agreed with the statement that God made the world. Nearly two-fifths (38 per cent) believed that Jesus is the Son of God and 21 per cent that he rose from the dead. One-half believed in reincarnation, but, like the Hindus, only 14 per cent believed that Mohammed is the Prophet of the one God. The Sikh teenagers had the highest proportion (40 per cent) who believed that Sikhism is the only true religion while only 1 per cent believed that Islam is the only true religion. These statistics reflect the fact that Sikhism has never been an exclusivist religion and has been open to assimilate ideas and practices from other traditions.[6]

13.4 Summary

The South Asian British teenagers were much more religious than the White British. Twice as many of them believed in God and there was a far higher level of belief that God punishes wrong, in life after death and that God is the creator of the world.

A minority of the non-affiliates held religious beliefs but their numbers were far fewer than those in the other groups. Compared with the other three religious groups, the adolescent Christians had smaller proportions who believed in God, that God punishes wrongdoing and in life after death. Of the religious groups, the Hindus had the smallest proportion who believed that God made the world and the least exclusivist views about their religion. The Muslims had the largest proportions who believed in God, that God punishes wrongdoing, in life after death and that God created the world. Levels of religious belief were highest among the teenage Muslims. The Sikh young people had relatively high levels of belief but did not exhibit a particularly distinctive profile.

14
Conclusions and recommendations

14.1 Introduction

In Western societies great stress is placed on ethnicity as the most important key to understand and interpret the lives of people and communities. In this book, however, it has been argued that identification with religious groups must be taken equally seriously as a factor. This has implications for:

- planners and commissioners of health services;
- people who deliver health services;
- those who are engaged with health promotion and health education;
- agencies concerned with tobacco, alcohol and drug abuse;
- professionals working within the education sector;
- employers seeking to recruit and employ young people;
- policy-makers;
- politicians.

The secularization of society in some parts of the West has led to a consistent underestimation and trivialization of the impact of religious beliefs among many people in the United Kingdom. Consequently, some politicians and commentators in Britain were taken by surprise at the responses of some members of the Muslim community to the Salman Rushdie affair and more recently the attack on the World Trade Centre on 11 September 2001. Why were we surprised at this? The work of Francis and others (as described in the introduction) has demonstrated clearly the influence that Christian beliefs have on a wide range of attitudes and values. The research detailed in this book has confirmed their findings and shown that the same is true for Hindus, Muslims and Sikhs.

A study of the history of immigration into Britain shows that in the past most peoples have been gradually assimilated and their distinctive identities have become diluted over a period of time. Perhaps the main exception to this has been those of the Jewish faith, although even here the situation may be changing. The major difference in the contemporary situation is the size of the immigrant population which is so much larger than any movements of population in recent times. This means that different groups retain their distinctive cultural and religious identity for much longer. As one would expect, this piece of research has shown that some Hindu, Muslim and Sikh adolescents have been influenced by the prevailing British culture and that a significant minority do not practise their faith. Despite this, there are other, perhaps equally strong, forces pulling in the opposite direction. For example, Nielsen (2000: 124) has commented on the way that some young British Muslims have increasingly identified themselves with the wider Muslim world (*umma*) in recent years and that many more of them are now learning Arabic, whilst Ballard (2000: 143) has recently concluded 'that there are no indications that British Sikhs are losing their sense of distinctiveness'. Indeed, religion is considered to have played a part in the series of riots which took place in a number of towns and cities in the Midlands and north of England during the summer of 2001, and more recently in Birmingham in 2005.

These issues are likely to increase in importance since demographic studies show that whilst the birth rate among the white population has continued to fall, the birth rate among the South Asian British population remains much higher.[1] It is inevitable that the size of the South Asian British community will grow for many years and will become an increasingly important part of British society.

14.2 Islam in Britain

Whether Christian, Hindu, Muslim or Sikh, religion is a significant factor for many young people growing up in Britain today. What is absolutely clear from this research is that Muslims have the most distinctive profile. Seven features of teenage Muslims stood out in particular.

Firstly, they expressed the highest levels of trust of people in authority. For example, they had the largest proportion who thought that teachers and the local council did a good job; and had the second highest proportion who trusted the police. More of them thought that state ownership of industry was a good thing and more of them had confidence in political parties (both Conservative and Labour). This suggests that young Muslims have a more hierarchical, less egalitarian, view of society than other groups.

Second, more of them held conservative views on sexual morality and disapproved of divorce, contraception, under-age sexual intercourse, extramarital sex and homosexuality. Third, in a number of areas they appeared to be more confident and positive than the teenagers in the other groups. For example, a larger proportion of them thought that life had a purpose and a smaller proportion of them were concerned what other people thought about them or had experienced jealousy of others. As a group they were also the least reluctant to discuss their problems with professionals. They were more purposeful in their use of leisure time. Fourth, they had a strong sense of personal right and wrong. Compared with the other groups, fewer claimed that they lied or took advantage of other people and more of them were against getting drunk and smoking cigarettes (although they did not have particularly strong views on the use of cannabis, heroin and glue sniffing). More of them thought there was too much television violence and pornography. Sixth, they were the group that was most concerned about the growth of unemployment in their area and they had the highest proportion who would rather be unemployed than do a job that they did not like. Fewer of them were worried about being unemployed. Lastly, more of them held religious beliefs, such as belief in God, that God punishes wrongdoing, that God created the world, and in life after death.

This strong sense of identity in the Muslim community is directly linked to levels of social capital (see chapter 1). However, social capital can be either good or bad. It can inspire, for example, generous charitable giving (*zakat*) by sending money home to the areas from which their families originated, or it can create a culture which inspires young men to fly aeroplanes into the Twin Towers in New York. The challenge for all communities, religious or secular, not least the Muslim community following the Twin Towers disaster of 11 September 2001, is whether their strong and distinctive community identity and shared beliefs will be an expression of bonding social capital or bridging social capital.[2]

14.3 Taking religion seriously as part of the public agenda

Some professions acknowledge that a person's stated religion may be relevant to the way services are provided for them, and that there needs to be a degree of sensitivity or awareness of the professional providing a service for that person or group. At a superficial level, this has required awareness of the particular religious customs or beliefs of an individual.

For some considerable time, collection of data about a person's religious affiliation has been the norm in settings such as hospitals, schools and prisons. In fact, the data has been routinely requested for much longer than the ethnic background of individuals, which has now come to the fore in the light of race relations legislation. More public services are also making diversity-awareness training mandatory for their employees. Whilst it can be argued that these actions may amount to nothing more than paying lip-service to the issues that this presents, it does reinforce to professionals that each person's behaviour, needs and expectations are influenced by a whole range of factors and these will inevitably affect the way services should be delivered and may be received.

A particular example is the series of books produced by Henley (1983a, 1983b, 1983c) that aim to help health professionals when they are caring for people of different religious groupings. This sort of information is useful in highlighting particular rituals or customs associated with situations such as dying and death.

However, the importance of religion is more profound and pervasive than simply being sensitive to a person's religion and customs. Religion touches on many deep-seated attitudes and assumptions which people make. Without an awareness of these issues not only may we fail to understand significant differences between the various religious groups, but more importantly, serious mistakes may be made in social policy, and resources may be wasted because they have not been carefully and accurately targeted. This may be illustrated from eight areas of this research.

14.3.1 Implications for commissioners of health services

The responsibility for planning and commissioning services to meet the health needs of the population rests with primary care trusts. To do this, they are required under legislation to work in partnership with other statutory agencies, such as social services departments of local authorities, police, education and housing and environmental health departments. Local strategic partnerships have now been set up across the country to enable these organizations to meet their responsibilities for planning and working together to meet the needs of the local population.

Directors of public health have a key role in identifying the health needs of the population served by each primary care trust. These health needs assessments help to inform the commissioning plans, and the allocation of resources described in the local delivery plans which each primary care trust is required to develop.

A wide range of demographic factors are taken into account in undertaking the health needs assessment of their population. To do this, public health teams rely heavily on population census data which, combined with figures on incidence and prevalence of particular conditions, help to identify the services which will need to be commissioned. Until the 2001 census, information on religious affiliation was not collected. Whilst the actual incidence and prevalence of a significant number of diseases and conditions will be related to racial origins, it is universally recognized that environmental factors also play a significant role, along with motivation and behaviour. The religious affiliation of a primary care trust's population may therefore have a marked influence not only on the type of services which are to be commissioned, but also on the way that the services are delivered. If planning and resource allocation is based purely on ethnicity, as reported in table 4.3, one approach would be pursued for all the White British within a given population and another undifferentiated approach for the South Asian British teenagers.

This research has clearly demonstrated that a more subtle approach should be taken, particularly in respect of populations where there are a significant number of young people within an area expressing affiliation to the Hindu or Muslim faith (table 4.4). Compared with the other groups, far more Hindu adolescents indicated that they wanted advice but fewer of them were willing to discuss their problems with a professional. Further research may be needed to discover the reasons for this. Nonetheless, it would appear that other resources may need to be developed to support this group of people in addition to the existing provision through health and social care professionals and other statutory organizations. Increasingly, peer counselling, 'buddying' and mentoring are being used with young people and are being found to be more successful in giving support where efforts from professionals have failed. An example of an alternative approach began in January 2006 when a hate-crime hotline was set up for Hindus following the London bombings in July 2005. As well as dealing with complaints it will also offer victim support (*The Times*, 4 January 2006). However, this will deal only with a small number of the concerns expressed by the teenage Hindus.

14.3.2 Implications for those delivering health services

The implications of this research and analysis are considerable when assessing the impact on the delivery of health services. Although overall this age group is not a major user of health services compared to, for example, young children and the elderly, there are some specific health services which are particularly relevant. These include primary mental health services and sexual health promotion. Primary health care teams, and in particular general practitioners, practice nurses and school nurses are often seen to be the first professionals to be approached for health advice and support. The research has shown, however, that this is the case for only a small number of young people. The data has shown that they are less likely to use other forms of support as well. Primary health care workers need to make more strenuous attempts to understand why some young people are reluctant to use their services and ensure that the teams are representative of the populations they serve in respect of ethnic and religious mix. They may also need to look at ways of providing the services closer to where these young people are likely to congregate, including faith-based youth clubs.

Those health professionals with a responsibility to promote family planning and to provide guidance in the case of those trying to avoid pregnancy or seeking abortions ought to be aware that a significantly higher percentage (21 per cent) of Muslims thought that contraception is wrong, compared with only 4 per cent of the Hindu and 6 per cent of the Sikh adolescents. Over three-fifths of the Muslims thought that abortion is wrong, compared with 25 per cent of the Hindus and 39 per cent of the Sikhs (table 5.4). These contrasting figures are not to be dismissed, or simply placed under the amorphous all-purpose category 'cultural'. Further research, studying the statistics about unwanted pregnancies among teenage girls from the main religious communities, may well shed light on the importance of such insights and help scarce resources be targeted more effectively.

14.3.3 Implications for those planning and providing health promotion and health education

The responses of the South Asian British teenagers to the statements on sexual morality need careful assimilation if they are to be used to develop effective health promotion and health education material for this group. The stark differences between the responses based on ethnicity and religion illustrate this. Of the South Asian British teenagers, 40 per cent thought that it was wrong to have sexual intercourse outside marriage compared with 12 per cent of the White British. The figure of 40 per cent masks the very wide variations between the three South Asian British religions. Only 23 per cent of the Hindus thought that it was wrong compared with 56 per cent of the Muslims. These findings are also relevant to teachers and school governors who are responsible for deciding appropriate ways to deliver personal and social education (PSE). Many teachers feel ill-equipped to discuss sexual health mores with young people, and work in partnership with other professionals, such as school nurses, to deliver specific elements of the PSE curriculum. This is likely to be most challenging in a multi-faith school where there is be a wider range of beliefs and opinions than in a school for predominantly white British teenagers.

In their responses to most of the statements in the research relating to views about sexual behaviour, there are similarly large differences between the adolescent Hindus and Sikhs when compared with the Muslims. In the light of this, those working in sex education in schools may find it helpful to know that 57 per cent of the Muslims and 33 per cent of the Sikhs thought that sexual intercourse under the age of sixteen is wrong, and that 53 per cent of the Muslims and 22 per cent of the Sikhs thought that homosexuality is wrong. School counsellors need to be alert to the fact that young Muslims who get pregnant or who are wondering whether or not they are gay will probably need extra support since their community is likely to be not only more critical, but also by implication, less supportive.

14.3.4 Implications for those concerned with tobacco, alcohol and drug abuse

The fourth area where religion plays a significant part in forming attitudes relates to the purchase and use of tobacco, drugs and alcohol. When compared with the South Asian British, the proportion of the White British adolescents who thought that there was nothing wrong in buying cigarettes was 13 percentage points greater and the proportion who thought there was nothing wrong in buying alcohol under the legal age was 23 percentage points greater. When the data is re-examined in the light of the religious allegiance of the young people, the wide variation between the groups becomes clear. Only 17 per cent of the Hindus thought that there was nothing wrong in buying cigarettes under the legal age compared with 23 per cent of the Sikhs. Likewise, only 17 per cent of the Muslims thought that there was nothing wrong in buying alcohol under the legal age compared with 35 per cent of the Hindus.

The data obtained from comparing the White British with the South Asian British teenagers shows that 18 per cent of the former thought that it was wrong to become drunk compared with 50 per cent of the South Asian group. Nearly two-fifths (37 per cent) thought that it is wrong to smoke cigarettes compared with 50 per cent respectively. Once again, when the material is examined on the basis of religious affiliation a more complex picture emerges. The Muslim adolescents were the group with the largest proportion who thought that it is wrong to become drunk (70 per cent) compared with the Sikhs (30 per cent). Over half of the Muslims thought that is wrong to smoke cigarettes (55 per cent) compared with 42 per cent of the Sikhs. Agencies involved in the prevention of drug and alcohol abuse will find that research based on religion, as well as ethnicity, could allow them to focus their programmes more effectively by concentrating on those groups of young people who are most likely to start smoking. Research on peer support and education within the faith communities is worth further exploration in these areas.

It is worrying that in all five groups (the four religious groups and the non-affiliates) there was a considerable minority who did not think that it was wrong to sniff glue, or use cannabis or heroin. However, at the end of chapter 7, it was noted that, compared with the other religious groups and the non-affiliates, the Hindu teenagers were less likely to sniff glue, the Christians and Hindus were less likely to take cannabis, and the Christians, Hindus and Muslims were less likely to use heroin. In order to deploy resources most effectively, for example, in drug awareness campaigns, it is proposed that the non-affiliates groups should be the main target for action, along with Sikh adolescents, whilst Muslim teenagers would require proportionately less intensive targeting of resources.

14.3.5 Implications for professional groups working with the education sector

The fifth area where important and contrasting insights emerge is with regard to school and educational expectations. The findings of the research will therefore be of interest and relevance to teachers, education welfare officers, school governors and school counsellors. Some 77 per cent of the South Asian British teenagers said they were happy at school, although only 70 per cent of the Sikhs were happy compared with 86 per cent of the Hindus. However, 72 per cent of the South Asian British often worried about their school work, but only 69 per cent of the Muslims worried compared with 81 per cent of the Hindus. Teachers and educational counsellors need to be aware that the Sikh and Hindu teenagers are more likely to be unhappy at school and worried about their studies than their Muslim contemporaries. Despite this, it is significant that the group with the largest proportion who were worried about being bullied at school were the Muslim young people.

14.3.6 Implications for employers

Some significant differences may be found in the responses of the adolescents to the world of work, although in most instances the differences are relatively small. An exception to this are the differences between the White British and the South Asian British about having a job that one does not like or being on social security. One-fifth of the White British would rather be unemployed than do a job that they do not like, compared with one-quarter of the South Asian British. However, only 12 per cent of the Hindus agreed with this compared with 29 per cent of the Muslims.

In general, the response to the statement 'I would not like to be unemployed' was broadly the same for all teenagers, whatever their ethnic background. When the responses were divided into the four religious groups there was a statistically significant difference of $p<.001$. A smaller proportion of the Muslims indicated that they would not like to be unemployed (77 per cent) compared with the Christians (86 per cent), the Hindus (89 per cent) and the Sikhs (85 per cent). There are a wide number of factors which may influence whether a young person secures employment on leaving school, or becomes unemployed, such as the level of skills of the individual, mobility or institutionalized racism amongst employers. It is therefore not possible accurately to assess whether these beliefs translate into willingness or ability to secure paid employment upon leaving school. Nonetheless, employers and careers advisors may find these insights helpful in assessing the motives of future employees at interview.

It should be remembered that the young people used for this research were still at school. Whilst some of the older ones of the sample may have had part-time work outside school hours, and therefore some limited experience of the workplace, the results were not analysed by age groups, or experience of work. An interesting analysis would be to undertake a longitudinal study to assess whether the young people's views change once they are active within the workplace, and whether the differences between the groups of different religious affiliations are as marked then as they were when the young people were in the relatively more sheltered school environment.

14.3.7 Implications for policy-makers

The seventh area where important insights could be missed if the religious dimension is not taken into account is found in chapter 11 'Global and national concerns'. One-third of the South Asian British teenagers thought that there is too much violence on television, but this comprises 43 per cent of the Muslims compared with 21 per cent of the Sikhs. One of the greatest differences of attitude is found with regard to the National Lottery. More that two-fifths (43 per cent) of the South Asian British thought that it is a good thing, although only 28 per cent of the Muslims agreed with this compared with 61 per cent of the Sikhs.

14.3.8 Implications for politicians

Finally, if the data is analysed on the basis of religious affiliation it shows wide differences in support for the two main political parties. More of the young people had confidence in the Labour Party than in the Conservative Party, but the differences were marked between the religious groups. Only 4 per cent of the Sikhs compared with 15 per cent of the Muslims had confidence in the Conservative Party and 32 per cent of the Hindus compared with 48 per cent of the Muslims had confidence in the Labour Party. These contrasting profiles will be of major interest to politicians and political agents during campaigning among South Asian British voters living in their constituencies.

Significant differences also emerged between the groups of young people with differing religious affiliation in respect of state ownership of industry, immigration policy and even the effectiveness of the local authority. Although 22 per cent of the South Asian British teenagers thought that state ownership of industry is a good thing, only 10 per cent of the Hindus agreed, compared with 25 per cent of the Muslims. More than one-quarter (26 per cent) of the South Asian British adolescents thought that the local council does a good job. However, only 17 per cent of the Sikhs agreed, compared with 34 per cent of the Muslims. And although 17 per cent of the South Asian British teenagers thought that immigration into Britain should be restricted, there were differences between the Muslim community (19 per cent) and the Hindu community (10 per cent). These differences will be relevant to politicians when framing laws and policies concerning immigration.

Politicians and political agents, particularly in areas where there are significant numbers of young voters from South Asian British communities, would be well advised to consider possible reasons for these differences, and identify ways of engaging these young people more in local politics, particularly in the light of the apparent decline in participation in the democratic process. Only by doing this will politicians be able to claim they are truly representing the views of their constituents.

These eight areas illustrate the importance of research based on religious affiliation for many areas of social, educational and political policy in the United Kingdom today. They highlight the need for all people working within statutory or voluntary agencies to take religious affiliation into account because this may give valuable clues about a person's motivation, their beliefs about a range of topics relevant to their daily lives and the way they behave.

14.4 Further research

This research has mapped out some of the areas which merit further study. The present study is a snapshot in time and if the material is to be of maximum use, then similar studies will need to be undertaken in order to track the trends. The research needs extending in a number of ways. First, it will need to examine other groups as well as Christians, Hindus, Muslims and Sikhs. For example, future studies would benefit by including Jews and Buddhists. Secondly, it needs to examine some of the religious groups and movements within each religion. Francis and Kay have already examined this with their studies of Christianity where they have looked at the differences between Anglican, Roman Catholic and the Free Churches (Francis and Kay, 1995). Similarly, there are differences between members of other religions which are significant, perhaps the most important of which is between the *sunni* and *shi'ite* Muslims. Thirdly, research into the contrasting responses of males and females may provide important material for reflection, not least in predicting general trends in birth rates and participation in the labour market. Finally, it would be helpful to track some of adolescents as they grow older to see if there are significant changes in religious beliefs, values and attitudes over time, as Francis and Kay (1995) have found among adolescent Christians.

Appendix 1

The research method, the sample and the use of statistics

The Teenage Religion and Values Initiative developed a questionnaire that has been used extensively with more than 20,000 teenagers among pupils at year 9 and 10 (thirteen- to fifteen-year-olds) (Francis and Kay, 1995). The first section of Francis's questionnaire sought general information about each subject such as age, gender, academic aspirations at school, parental occupation, religious affiliation, attendance at public worship, prayer and religious experience.[1] The second section of Francis's questionnaire was a short Eysenck personality profile. The third section sought the views of the teenagers on a wide range of issues including religion, relationships, morality, leisure, school, work, global issues and politics. The final section asked those adolescents who considered themselves to be practising Christians a range of questions about their church, its leaders and their involvement in its life and activities.

Francis's questionnaire had been designed to research the beliefs of adolescent Christians and it did not include any material specifically for those of other faiths. Therefore one of the first tasks was to re-examine the questionnaire and to decide how it should be adapted. Some of the changes, such as the self-assignation into the different religious groups, were obvious. The adolescents were asked to answer the question 'Do you belong to a church or other religious group?' and they were given seven categories from which to choose: Christian, Buddhist, Hindu, Jewish, Muslim, Sikh or other. If they ticked 'other' they were asked to specify to which other religion they belonged.

Much more complex, however, was deciding which questions to ask about the practices of those of other religions, which were to be found in two different sections of the questionnaire. Some of these were in the main body of the questionnaire while others were in the optional sections at the end of the questionnaire for those who were practising their faith. In the light of the large amount of data that the Francis and Kay research had already collected, should the same statements be put to the Walsall adolescents so that comparisons could be made? Or, alternatively, should all the statements be completely reworked and extra ones be added, to allow for the South Asian British teenagers? If this latter course were followed then it would be more difficult to use the Francis and Kay material to make comparisons. It was decided to stick as closely as possible to the questions that had been used by Francis and Kay and then to develop additional question for those of faiths other than Christianity.

In order to compile the material for the final part of the questionnaire three separate meetings were held with Hindu, Muslim and Sikh religious leaders, parents and teenagers to discuss the areas of research, how to phrase the statements and questions, and even which words should be used and how they should be spelt. This proved to be a more complex process than had originally been envisaged. One of the difficulties that arose at this stage was that some people used different words to describe the same thing. This is because the words have been translated from another language or even from two other languages. Indeed, some of the adults spelt or pronounced the same words differently. Rather than always give what might technically be the correct transliteration of some words, it was decided to try to identify the words that the adolescents and their families used and follow their usage. Even this was not without its difficulties. For example, Nesbitt and Jackson (1993–4: 56; 1995: 108–20) have pointed out that even such words as 'God' are sometimes used in different ways, both semantically and grammatically.

A draft questionnaire was drawn up. Like Francis and Kay's questionnaire, it consisted of short, unambiguous statements or questions to which the pupils were asked to respond. The questionnaire, was piloted and then went through a further stage of refinement to test it (Wolf, 1997: 423–5). Consequently, in some cases a choice of terms or words was included where these were being used by the adolescents, or a spelling of a word which was nearer to the way that the Walsall adolescents pronounced it.

Using the questionnaire in the secondary schools in Walsall

The questionnaires were distributed and completed between June 1996 and March 1997. At the end of this time completed responses from 3,418 children were obtained. Two schools declined to take part due to pressure on their timetables, and despite repeated approaches another school did not get round to using the questionnaires, although they had initially agreed to do so.

Two problems emerged as the questionnaire was used. A minority of the adolescents were unable to complete the questionnaire because their reading ability was so low. The second problem encountered in the research was the small group of *Ravidasis* adolescents had to choose to self-assign themselves into either the Hindu or the Sikh category, when their religion draws on aspects of both faiths. Nesbitt (1990a, 9–12; 1990b, 261–74; 1991, 8–11 and 32; 1995: 34) studied *Valmiki* and *Ravidasi* children and came across this same problem, which McLeod (1989: 112) also noted. This problem was not appreciated when the questionnaire was being designed and later when it was used. Therefore caution must be exercised when interpreting the data, especially since the number of Hindus and Sikhs is relatively small. In the case of the description of their places of worship, the *Ravidasis* have been treated as Sikhs.

Once the questionnaires had been completed the data was entered onto a computer programme. The results were then checked by running them through the Statistical Package for Social Sciences (SPSS). This highlighted any inconsistencies and enabled the data to be checked before being used to draw any conclusions.

The schools involved and the sample

There are twenty secondary schools in Walsall. Only three schools were unwilling or unable to participate: Frank F. Harrison, Sneyd and Willenhall. There were approximately 7,762 children in year 9 and year 10, of whom 3,418 filled in questionnaires sufficiently well for them to be used (table A1.1). The sample turned out to be a good representation of both genders (table A1.2) and both school years (table A1.3).

Table A1.1 Secondary schools in Walsall

	Approximate number of pupils in the school	Approximate number of pupils in years 9 and 10	Number of pupils who completed the questionnaire	Percentage of year 9 and 10 pupils who completed the questionnaire
County comprehensives				
Alumwell	940	332	22	7
Brownhills	870	300	114	38
Darlaston	1,150	410	104	25
Frank F. Harrison	620	270	–	–
Joseph Leckie	910	320	217	68
Manor Farm	700	250	123	49
Pool Hayes	1,070	370	248	67
Shelfield	880	320	217	68
Sneyd	1,340	490	–	–
T. P. Riley	790	320	265	83
Willenhall	1,460	520	–	–
Voluntary aided comprehensives				
Blue Coat Church of England	1,020	360	283	79
St Francis of Assisi RC	1,010	360	213	59
Grant maintained				
Aldridge	1,450	480	253	53
Barr Beacon	1,340	470	348	74
Shire Oak	1,100	420	145	35
Streetly	1,120	390	177	45
St Thomas More RC	1,360	480	375	78
Queen Mary's Grammar (Boys)	650	200	136	68
Queen Mary's High (Girls)	660	200	178	89
Total	20,440	7,262	3,418	47

Table A1.2 The sample: gender

	Sample N	Percentage %
Male	1,656	48.5
Female	1,758	51.4
Failed to answer this question	4	0.1
	3,418	100.0

Table A1.3 The sample: year group

	Sample N	Percentage %
Year 9	1,800	52.7
Year 10	1,574	46.1
Failed to answer this question	44	1.3
	3,418	100.0

The use of statistics

Numbers have been rounded up or down to one decimal point, unless a source is being quoted which uses two or more decimal points. Where there is a percentage figure of less than 0.5 it has been recorded as <1. When noting statistical significance the convention of using three categories: $p<.05$, $p<.01$ and $p<.001$ has been used. This means that there are five times per hundred, one time per hundred and one time per thousand respectively when the results would be produced by random. Therefore it is important for the reader to exercise more caution over the results based on $p<.05$ than the results based on $p<.01$ and $p<.001$. The abbreviation NS stands for 'not significant' and means that the results could have arisen because of chance. Therefore, it is important not to place too much weight on such figures. As a general rule, I have not made any comments on those statistics which are statistically not significant.

Appendix 2

A note of nomenclature

A wide variety of terms have been used to describe the ethnic and racial groups in the United Kingdom. Many of these have changed over time and reflect different levels of self-understanding and political correctness (Banton, 1977: 480–2 and 1987: 170–5). Such terms include negro, black, coloured, New Commonwealth, immigrant, coloured immigrants, Indian, Pakistani, Bangladeshi and Asian. The way that the terminology has changed is illustrated by a letter in the *Walsall Observer*, 10 November 1989, in which Mr Tim Oliver, chairman of the Palfrey Labour Party, criticized the newspaper for 'using the language of the 1950s by referring to "coloured people".' Mason (1990: 123–33) examined a range of terms and concluded that no one set of terms proved fully adequate. Modood (1988: 397–404) was critical of the term 'black' to encompass all non-white ethnic groups and some years later Ranger, Samad and Stuart (1996: 1) argued that 'Blackness defined as the common experience of oppression by non-whites has given away to a myriad of externally imposed or self-asserted ethnicities'. Some authors have tried to leave open the terminology (Modood, Beishon and Virdee, 1994: 15), whilst others have adopted the terms which are now becoming most widely used, such as 'Asian British' or 'South Asian British' (Bald, 1989: 537). For the purposes of this book the term 'South Asian British' is used to describe those whose racial origins are in India, Pakistan and Bangladesh and who are living in the United Kingdom. I have used the term White British to describe those whose racial origins are in the United Kingdom.

Notes

Introduction

[1] A more detailed description of the initiative and the methodology of The Teenage Religion and Values Initiative can be found in Kay and Francis (1996: 159–200).

[2] Other researchers have noted the relationship between religion and substance abuse (Gorsuch, 1995) and religion and health (Matthews, McCullough, Larson, Koenig, Swyers and Milano, 1998).

[3] 'The nature and significance of religion among adolescents in the Metropolitan Borough of Walsall', thesis submitted for the degree of Doctor of Philosophy, University of Wales (Bangor) in 2002. Details of the methodology and sample can be found in Appendix 1.

Chapter 1: Britain: a nation in transition

[1] This was one of the findings of *Still No Idea* (2002). Teenagers and parents were asked what were the biggest problems the teenagers faced. Drugs were highlighted by 42 per cent of the parents and by 19 per cent of the teenagers. Relationships were a cause of concern for 28 per cent of the adults but 31 per cent of the young people. And 7 per cent of the adults thought that bullying was a problem compared with 13 per cent of the teenagers. None of the parents thought that mental health was a problem while 3 per cent of the teenagers were concerned about it. Commenting on these findings, Justin Irwin, director of Get Connected, said:

> Young people and drug related problems are rarely out of the media and this is one of the reasons that parents' concerns about drugs are totally out of proportion with the problem itself. It is almost as if some parents think that there are practically no other problems. Addressing the issue of drugs is important, but it must not be at the expense of dealing with other problems that young people face, particularly problems to do with mental health issues, which do not get such widespread media coverage. (*Still No Idea*, 2002: 7).

[2] The term was first coined by Hanifan in 1916 (quoted in Rae, 2002: xi). A number of scholars have offered definitions of social capital.

Bourdieu (1985: 248) suggested 'the aggregate of the actual or potential resources which are linked to possession of a durable network of more or less institutionalized relationships of mutual acquaintance or recognition'. Hall (1999: 417) defined it as 'the propensity of individuals to associate together on a regular basis, to trust one another, and to engage in community affairs', whilst Putnam has offered several different definitions, for example, 'features of social organization, such as trust, norms, and networks, that can improve the efficiency of society by facilitating coordinated actions' (1993: 167), 'features of social life – networks, norms, and trust – that enable participants to act more effectively to pursue shared objectives' (1996: 34) and 'connections among individuals – social networks and the norms of reciprocity and trustworthiness that arise from them' (2000: 19).

3. Leach (1999) pointed out that there was a fall in charitable donations from £5.3 billion in 1995 to £4.5 billion in 1997 in the United Kingdom. Pharoah and Tanner (1997: 427–43) have also pointed out falls in charitable giving and also the phenomenon that younger people are not donating as much as older people. However, there are signs in some areas that levels of charitable giving are holding steady, for example, the speech by Stephen Ainger at the Charities Aid Foundation conference in 2004 (http://www.cafonline.org/conference/speech04ainger.cfm) and the 2002 report from the National Council for Voluntary Organizations (http://www.ncvo-vol.org.uk).

4. For a discussion about the use of the term 'South Asian British', see appendix 2.

5. For example, the average age of the population is forty-one but the average age of the Muslim population is twenty-eight. For a detailed age breakdown of the population according to religion, see Peach, 2005: 25.

6. The areas with the highest proportion of ethnic groups are in Leicester, Bradford, Tower Hamlets, Lewisham, Hackney and Harrow.

7. For a fuller description of urban rioting, see Bagguely and Hussain, 2005.

8. Modood, commenting on this issues, noted 'Industrial tribunal cases have been based on the right of Asian women to wear *shalwar-kamiz*, Rastafarian men to wear dreadlocks at work and Muslim women the *hijab* (respectively, *Malik v. British Home Stores* 1980; *Dawkins v. Crown Supplies* 1989; and *Shakoor v. Anne Gray Associates* 1960) (Modood, 1997: 326).

9. An article in *The Times* on 15 April 2004 described the way that many young Muslims are becoming Westernized and a minority are becoming radicalized.

10. *The Sunday* Times (28 July 2002) ran a newspaper article examining the links of young South Asian British men with terrorists. The

Notes 139

transformation of South Asian British young men into radical Muslims is examined in an article in *The Times*, 2 April 2004. There were also reports that South Asian British men had enlisted to fight in the conflict around the mosque in Najaf in August 2004 (*The Times*, 12 August 2004).

11 Similar events have been reported in other European countries, such as the stoning to death of Ghofrane Haddaoui in Marseilles (*The Times*, 4 December 2004).

12 For example, Wilson (1966; 1976), Berger (1969), Martin (1969; 1978), Acquaviva (1979), Lechner (1991; 1996), Tschannen (1991) and Bruce (1996).

13 Ghuman (1994: 68–9) asked fifty Asian adolescents how they would choose to describe their identity. The vast majority chose to use religious rather than ethnic categories.

14 Hutnik (1991: 88–91), Modood, Beishon and Virdee (1994: 62), Knott and Khokher (1993: 605), Nesbitt and Jackson (1993–4: 57), The Home Office (2004: 26).

Chapter 2: The religious affiliation and practices of teenagers in Britain

1 The 2001 census found that one in ten Muslims in Britain described themselves as of white origin. The census revealed that there were 1,546,626 Muslims in Britain, of which 179,773 said that they were white. Of these 63,042 were British, 890 were Irish and 115,841 were 'other' whites.

2 Fane quoted a paper produced for the *2001 Census of Population and Dwellings in New Zealand*, which asserted that the 'practical value of census information on religion is questionable, particularly in view of the fact that it does not provide an accurate indication of either the church-going practices of the population or the depth of a person's commitment to their specified religion' (Fane, 1999: 115). In her article Fane examined the problems with this approach but concluded 'There is evidence, then, to suggest that religious affiliation is, in its own right, socially significant' (p. 117) and 'Self-assigned religious affiliation may be useful as a predictor of other markers of religiosity such as practice and belief, particularly when divided by denomination, but self-assigned religious affiliation may also be useful as a predictor of social attitudes and behaviours . . .' (p. 122).

Chapter 3: Well-being and mental health

1 For example, *Observer*, 19 May 2002; *Guardian Unlimited*, 5 September 2004.

2 See http://www.suicidereferencelibrary.com/424.html and also the figures released by the Samaritans in 1992 which showed that the

number of suicides among men aged fifteen to twenty-four in England and Wales had increased from 262 in 1982 (a rate of six deaths per 100,000) to 412 in 1992 (a rate of eleven per 100,000).
3 *London Evening Standard*, 28 January 2004.
4 *The Times* (18 November 2004) reported research published in *Archives of Disease in Childhood* which showed that there was a 70 per cent rise in prescribing antidepressants between 1992 and 2001 in Britain, providing medication to 25,000 young people up to the age of eighteen years old.
5 Woodroffe et al., 1993.
6 Frances and Lester (1997); Francis and Katz (2002); Francis and Robbins (2000); Demir and Urberg (2004).
7 NS is an abbreviation for 'not significant' and refers to a statistical test which indicates that one needs to be cautious in placing too much weight on such statistics. For further details turn to the final section of appendix 1.
8 Verma and Bagley (1975: 230), Louden (1978a: 226; 1978b: 207; 1980: 27), Bagley, Mallick and Verma (1979: 190), Field (1984: 12), Verma and Ashworth (1986: 185), Verma and Mallick (1988, 160–1), Hutnik (1991: 75–6, 145).

Chapter 4: Relating to other people

1 *The Times*, 30 December 2002. Other researchers have also found that parents and teenagers see things differently. For example, Simmons and Wade (1984: 76), Fogelman (1976: 36), Willmott (1966: 61–2) and Noller and Callan (1991: 86).
2 *The Times*, 8 October 2004.
3 The Commission for Racial Equality Report (1978: 17) discovered that about one in three of all the Asians surveyed were living in extended families and two-thirds were living in nuclear households. Owen (1996: 15), commenting on the 1991 census, noted that, while the average household in Britain contained 2.47 people, there were on average 4.2 people in Asian households. There were also likely to be more adults in Asian households: 'While 31 per cent of white households contained only one adult, 25.4 per cent of households with a head from an ethnic minority contained three or more adults' (Owen, 1996: 16). Only one-tenth of Asian families were single-parent families, compared with 13 per cent of white families. Clearly Asian adolescents have more adults in their homes to whom they can turn for advice if they wish. Anwar (1998: 102), quoting figures from the 1991 census, showed that Asians were much more likely than white people to live in houses containing at least two families and that these families were more likely to be extended, not just nuclear families.

4 Saeed and Galbraith asked seventy-nine Asian boys and twenty-one Asian girls to respond to the statement 'It is enjoyable to live in a large family with aunts and uncles'. The boys responded with 43 agreeing, 28 disagreeing, 2 who were neutral and 6 who did not know. The girls were less positive with 9 agreeing, 10 disagreeing and 2 who neither agreed or disagreed (1981/2: 449).
5 Beetham found that parental influence was much more important among Asians than West Indians and whites when it came to choosing a job: 'The aspirations of immigrant children, then, seems to derive largely from the aspiration their parents have for them' (1967: 20).
6 Brah discovered that the experience of Asian fifth-form adolescents varied:

> There was thus considerable variation in the quality of communication with parents as reported by these teenagers. Only four respondents (two boys and two girls) expressed resentment against parents with whom their relationships, especially with the father, were far from amicable. In two of these cases, the fathers appeared to be authoritarian and traditional (Brah, 1978: 204).

Brah suggested that the difficulties of communication may be because 'certain features of the children's socialisation outside school are beyond their [the parents] own range of experience' (Brah, 1979: 279).
7 They compared 'British' and Asian parents and adolescents by asking them whom they confided in most frequently and whom they put first on their list.
8 According to the Office for National Statistics, the average size of Muslim households was 3.8 people, compared with 3.6 (Sikh) and 3.2 (Hindu). Jewish, Christian and Buddhist households were smaller (http://www.statistics.gov.uk/cci/nugget.asp?id=961).
9 One such story was reported in *The Times* on 6 March 2004 when Aisha (her surname was not given), aged seventeen, was repatriated from Pakistan by the British High Commission. She had gone to Pakistan for a funeral, only to find that it had been arranged for her to meet a prospective husband. The High Commission reported had dealt with eighty similar cases in the previous year.

Chapter 5: Sexual morality

1 Further disquiet has been expressed at the doubling in the number of cases of HIV in Britain between 1998 and 2003 (*The Times*, 25 November 2004). The Health Protection Agency reports regularly on the increasing incidence of sexually transmitted diseases: (http://www.hpa.org.uk/).
2 Such disagreements occasionally hit the news, for example, an article in *The Times*, 7 January 2006 entitled 'Gay, Muslim and trying to come

out of the closet'. In early 2006 Gay Muslims protested that they had been excluded from a government-sponsored Festival of Muslim Cultures in Sheffield (*The Guardian*, 23 January 2006).

Chapter 6: Questions of right and wrong
1. http://www.homeoffice.gov.uk/rds/pdfs05/hosb2005.pdf
2. Quoted in Richardson, R. (ed.) with Muir, H. and Smith, L. (2004).

Chapter 7: Substance use and abuse
1. 'Use of cannabis is clearly related to age – nearly four in ten of those aged between 18 and 34 have tried cannabis, compared with less than three per cent of those aged 55 and over' (Gould, Shaw and Ahrendt, 1996: 99).
2. An article in *The Sunday Times* (15 August 2004) reported research showing that 14- to 15-year-old girls were drinking and smoking more than their male counterparts.
3. European Monitoring Centre for Drugs and Drug Addiction: http://ar2005.emcdda.eu.int/en/elements/fig25-en.html
4. As well as age, Gould, Shaw and Ahrendt found that attitudes towards cannabis were affected by the stage at which a person finished their education (the earlier they left school, the greater the proportion against it), their political affiliation (a higher proportion of Conservatives were against legalization than Labour) and those who had a religious affiliation.
5. DeWitt (1969: 30), Tinker (1977: 180), Agnihotri (1987: 56), Drury (1991: 395 and 1996: 101) and Modood, Beishon and Virdee (1994: 51).
6. Department of Education and Science (1967: 17), Henley (1983b: 43) and Singh (1992: 10).

Chapter 8: Free time and leisure pursuits
1. The research took place in Manchester and Sheffield and involved four focus groups, 28 one-and-a-half-hour discussions with 178 people and interviews with 89 teenagers aged 13–15 (1996: 91).
2. For example, Cross (1976/7: 489–94), Brah (1978: 204) and Verma and Darby (1994: 131–4).
3. Harris Research Centre, 1993: 9; Field and Haiken, 1971: 94, Saeed and Galbraith, 1981/2: 449–50.
4. Livingstone (1977: 51–4) found that fewer Hindu adolescents joined clubs than Muslims or Sikhs, with the exception of out-of-school clubs (41 per cent), whilst more played with their friends (30 per cent).
5. Joly (1995: 57, 180), The National Association of Young Muslims Newsletter (5, 1985), and *The Muslim News*, 33, November 1991.

6 Hewitt (1993: 37–40), Lewis (1994: 181), Baily (1990: 153–5). However, research shows that music is very important to teenage Muslims (Banjeri and Bauman, 1990; 137–52).
7 Kalra (1980: 63), Helweg (1979: 119), Tatla (1993b: 120–2) and Singh (1992: 25).

Chapter 9: Education and schools

1 Hargreaves found that 74 per cent liked school (1967: 52). Fogelman (1976: 51) reported that 55 per cent disagreed with the statement 'I don't like school' and 30 per cent agreed. Hendry, Shucksmith, Love and Glendinning (1993: 79) found that among the boys 69 per cent of the thirteen- to fourteen-year-olds and 59 per cent of the fifteen- to sixteen-year-olds liked being at school compared with 82 per cent and 69 per cent of the girls respectively.
2 Field (1984: 25), Brah (1979: 297, 369) and Drew, Gray and Sime (1992: 10).
3 Brooks and Singh (n.d: 16) discovered that the Asian youths were more likely to stay in full-time education after the minimum leaving age than the white teenagers, indicating the high value they placed on education. Gupta (1977: 189) found a similar pattern. He also asked them about their intentions and wishes for higher education after leaving school and found that a much larger proportion of the South Asians had higher educational aspirations (p. 190). These results were in line with those of Beetham (1966), Taylor (1973a and 1973b), Penn and Scattergood (1992: 84) and Drew, Gray and Sime (1992: 25–30).
4 The relatively higher levels of academic aspiration were also found by Hilton (1972: 80), Fowler, Littlewood and Madigan (1977: 69–70), Swann (1985: 113), Jones (1993: 34–5), Drew (1995: 92) and Department for Education and Employment (1997: 18; 1998: 14; 1999a: 16; 1999b: 13). Summarizing the PSI research, Jones (1993: 154) wrote:

> Both Pakistani and Bangladeshi young people are more likely than whites to stay in full-time education after age 16. However, in terms of overall educational attainment they still lag far behind. The Pakistanis and Bangladeshis are by some way the least likely groups to hold formal qualifications. This is especially true for women of whom high proportions have never received any formal education at all.

5 Iqbal (1975), Kanitkar (1979), Nagra (1981/2), McLean (1985), Joly (1988), Halstead (1986, 1988), Hiskett (1989), Sarwar (1989, 1994), Modood (1997: 325).

6. Saifullah-Khan (1974: 296–8), Butterworth (1969: 149), Shaikh and Kelly (1989: 17–118), Joly (1995: 119–25).
7. http://www.statistics.gov.uk/cci/nugget.asp?id=963
8. Indeed, during the late 1980s concern was expressed in the newspapers that children were routinely being beaten at one of the mosques in Walsall (*Walsall Advertiser*, 8.1.87; *Evening Mail*, 6.1.87; *Walsall Observer*, 6.1.87).
9. This is backed by in research by Bhachu of the East African Sikh community (1985: 5–7, 20; 1991: 78).

Chapter 10: Work and employment

1. For example, Anwar (1998: 60) found that there are significant differences between the unemployment levels of Indians, Pakistanis and Bangladeshis.
2. Beetham (1967: 17, 22), Hilton (1972: 80), Fowler, Littlewood and Madigan (1977: 70–3), Hasnie (1977: 26), Gupta (1977, 188–92), Kannan (1978: 77), Murray and Dawson (1983: 34), Penn and Scattergood (1992: 75, 84), Ghuman (1999: 91–3).
3. For example, the Runnymede Trust (1974/5: 20); McGrath (1976: 244); Field, Mair, Rees and Stevens (1981: 33); Brah (1986: 63); Drew, Gray and Sime (1992: 51–2); Owen (1996: 31, 33).
4. For example, Jones (1981/2: 470–1); Robinson and Flintoff (1982: 255); Sills, Tarpey and Golding (1983: 40); Brooks (1983: 53).
5. Ghuman's sample was small (N=50) so caution should be exercised in using these figures.
6. Modood *et al* (1997: 113–14) found differences in earnings and job discrimination and also showed that 'the Hindus have the highest and Muslims the lowest rate of self-employment, Muslims being only three-quarters as likely to be in self-employment as non-Muslim Asians' (1997: 123).

Chapter 11: Global and national concerns

1. *Walsall Observer*, 21.5.93, 19.11.93.
2. *Walsall Observer*, 22.1.93, 9.2.93, 2.4.93, 16.4.93, 28.5.93, 4.6.93, 18.6.93, 20.8.93, 27.8.93, 10.9.93, 24.9.93, 8.10.93, 29.10.93, 4.2.94, 11.2.94, 25.3.94, 1.4.94, 22.4.94, 8.7.94, 22.7.94, 29.7.94, 16.9.94, 28.4.95, 12.5.95.
3. *Walsall Observer*, 21.1.94, 15.4.94.
4. For further explanation of statistical significance see appendix 1.
5. Express and Star, 16.7.92.

Chapter 12: Young people and politics

1. The first Asian candidate in local elections in Walsall was Mr Mohsi Jaffri in 1971 (*Walsall Observer*, 26 March 1971) who stood for Labour.

The first reference in local newspapers to any Asians being involved in the Conservative Party was in 1988 when the St Matthew's Conservative Association elected its first Asian chairman (*Walsall Observer*, 19 February 1988).
2 Hiro (1991: 172), Anwar (1994b: 21ff).
3 Le Lohé (1989: 160–1), Geddes (1993: 51–4).
4 Studlar (1983: 92–100), Anwar (1994b: 35ff).
5 Eade (1989: 46–8; 1992: 44), Joly (1995: 94).
6 Eade (1989: 47–8), Hiro (1991: 171), Eade (1992: 41).
7 John (1969: 123), James (1974: 93–4), Tatla (1993a: 97).
8 Hiro (1972: 129–30), Tatla (1993a: 97).
9 Drury (1996: 105) noted that many of the Sikh girls in her study had become more interested in Indian politics after the storming of the temple at Amritsar in 1984.

Chapter 13: Religious beliefs in the contemporary world

1 Similar sorts of questions have been used in a variety of surveys in recent years, with a wide range of responses. The 1985 Gallup survey found that 57 per cent of sixteen- to nineteen-year-olds claimed to believe in God (Heald and Wybrow, 1986: 262). Furnham and Gunter asked the twelve- to twenty-two-year-olds in their research if they believed in God or some other supernatural being. They found that 26 per cent believed 'in the existence of a higher force which has some influence over events in their lives' (Furnham and Gunter, 1989: 132). Inglehart (1990: 190–1) reported that 67 per cent of the fifteen- to twenty-four-year-olds in Britain said they believed in God, although only 34 per cent described themselves as 'a religious person'. Timms (1992: 69) found that 45 per cent of the eighteen- to twenty-five-year-olds said that they believed in God. In another piece of research 58 per cent of the twelve- to nineteen-year-olds believed in God (Roberts and Sachdev, 1996: 131). The differences in responses are most easily ascribed, at least in part, to the particular wording of the various statements which could lead them to be open to differing interpretation. Another consideration is the age difference of the respondents to the various pieces of research.
2 Two surveys found that 33 per cent of adolescents believed in life after death (Furnham and Gunter, 1989: 133; Heald and Wybrow, 1986: 262). Timms (1992: 69) found a slightly higher level (36 per cent) amongst a group of eighteen- to twenty-five-year-olds a few years later.
3 The 1985 Gallup survey found that 19 per cent of the sixteen- to nineteen-year-olds believed in reincarnation (Heald and Wybrow, 1986: 262).
4 This is in line with other findings such as Sigelman (1977: 290), quoting Gallup polls taken in a number of countries in 1975. In response to

146 Notes

the question 'Do you believe in God or a universal spirit?', 76 per cent of the British agreed. Interestingly this compared with the respondents from India where 98 per cent agreed.

5 Part of the reason for this apparent confusion may be due to the cross-fertilization of ideas in the teaching of religious education and in school assemblies. In the Commission for Racial Equality report (1978: 21) the young Asians were asked if they thought that they were influenced by Christianity through attending assemblies at school with a Christian assembly. The results indicate that 41 per cent thought that they were being influenced by the assemblies, but 48 per cent disagreed.

6 As Singh noted, 'It is not unusual to find a glittering Christmas tree in the front room of many Sikh households; the exchange of Christmas greeting cards between Sikh families is rather more common that that of Diwala or Gurpurb greeting cards' (1992: 40).

Chapter 14: Conclusions and recommendations

1 As well as Tables 14.1 and 14.2 on the facing page, see also the report by Migrationwatch (*The Times*, 5 January 2006) and the article 'Chinese become the fastest growing ethnic group' in *The Times*, 27 January 2006.

2 Bonding social capital is that which builds mutual commitment between members of a group. Whilst it can offer support to its members, it can also be exclusive and lead to antagonism to those who do not belong. In contrast, bridging social capital helps people to move beyond their own family or group and to engage with the stranger. It is, by definition, inclusive. Putnam (2000: 22) described it as follows:

> Of all the dimensions along which forms of social capital vary, perhaps the most important is the distinction between *bridging* (or inclusive) and *bonding* (or exclusive). Some forms of social capital are, by choice or necessity, inward looking and tend to reinforce exclusive identities and homogeneous groups. Examples of bonding social capital include ethnic fraternal organization, church-based women's reading groups, and fashionable country clubs. Other networks are outward looking and encompass people across diverse social cleavages. Examples of bridging social capital include the civil right movement, many youth service groups, and ecumenical religious organizations.

Appendix 1: The research method, the sample and the use of statistics

1 Fundamental to this approach to using a questionnaire is self-assigned religious affiliation, a method whereby the respondents are asked to specify to which religion they belong. Self-assignation as a tool has been

Table 14.1 Population size, per cent distribution by age and median age by ethnic group, 1997–1999, Great Britain

Years	Black Caribbean	Black African	Black other (non-mixed)	Black mixed	Indian	Pakistani	Bangladeshi	Chinese
Population distribution by age (%)								
0–14	22	31	41	58	23	34	40	16
15–29	19	26	27	25	24	31	29	31
30–44	30	31	28	13	27	20	18	31
45–64	14	9	2	3	16	10	8	14
65–74	13	3	2	1	8	6	6	7
75+	2	0	0	0	2	1	0	2
Median	33	26	18	11	31	22	18	31

Years	Other Asian (non-mixed)	Other other (-non mixed)	Other mixed	All minority ethnic groups	White	Total
Population distribution by age (%) continued						
0–14	21	27	52	30	19	19
15–29	23	23	23	25	19	20
30–44	34	31	15	25	23	23
45–64	16	14	7	12	19	19
65–74	5	3	2	6	14	13
75+	1	1	1	1	7	7
Median	32	29	12	26	37	36

Source: Scott, Pearce and Goldblatt (2000: 11)

Table 14.2 Growth of Britain's South Asian population, 1961–2001

Country of birth/ethnicity	1961	1971	1981	1991	2001
India	81,400	240,730	673,704	823,821	1,053,411
Pakistan	24,900	127,565	295,461	449,646	747,285
Bangladesh	–	–	64,562	157,881	283,063
East Africa	–	44,860	181,321	–	
Black	–	–	–	–	1,148,738
Total South Asian population	106,300	413,155	1,215,048	1,431,348	2,202,149
% South Asians in UK population	0.23	0.85	2.52	3.04	3.74

Source: Ballard (1994a: 7) and updated from the National Statistics Online (http://www.statistics.gov.uk/cci/nugget.asp?id=273)

questioned by some scholars (for example, White, 1979: 333–49), although it has continued to be used when ascertaining ethnicity in most censuses. However, there is an additional problem with religious self-assignation, namely nominalism, whereby a person may claim a religious allegiance whilst rarely or never attending public worship or even necessarily believing in even the most basic of the tenets of that religion. Fane (1999) examined this problem for the 2001 census. Her conclusions are described in chapter 2 (note 2).

Bibliography

ABC Television (1965). *Television and Religion*, London: London University Press.
Abrams, M., Gerard, D. and Timms, N. (eds), (1985). *Values and Social Change in Britain*, The European Value Systems Study Group, Basingstoke: Macmillan.
Acquaviva, S. S. (1979). *The Decline of the Sacred in Industrial Society*, Oxford: Basil Blackwell.
Afshar, H. (1989). 'Gender roles and the 'moral economy of kin' among Pakistani women in West Yorkshire', *New Community*, 15 (2), 211–26.
Agnihotri, R. K. (1987). *Crisis of Identity: The Sikhs in England*, New Delhi: Bahri Publications.
Ahrendt, D. and Young K. (1994). 'Authoritarianism updated', in R. Jowell, J. Curtice, L. Brook and D. Ahrendt with A. Park (eds), *British Social Attitudes, the 11th report*, Social and Community Planning Research, Aldershot: Dartmouth Publishing Company, pp. 75–93.
Anwar, M. (1994a). *Young Muslims in Britain: Attitudes, Eucational Needs and Policy Implications*, Leicester: The Islamic Foundation.
Anwar, M. (1994b). *Race and Elections: The Participation of Ethnic Minorities in Politics*, Coventry: Centre for Research in Ethnic Relations, University of Warwick.
Anwar, M. (1995). 'Social networks of Pakistanis in the UK: a re-evaluation', in A. Rogers and S. Vertovec (eds), *The Urban Context: Ethnicity, Social Networks and Situational Analysis*, Oxford: Berg Publishers, pp. 237–57.
Anwar, M. (1998). *Between Cultures: Continuity and Change in the Lives of Young Asians*, London and New York: Routledge.
Anwar, M. (2005). 'Issues, policy and practice', in T. Abbas (ed.), *Muslim Britain: Communities under Pressure*, London: Zed Books, pp. 31–46.
Bagguley, P. and Hussain, Y. (2005). 'Flying the Flag for England? Citizenship, religion and cultural identity among British Pakistani Muslims', in T. Abbas (ed.), *Muslim Britain: Communities under Pressure*, London: Zed Books, pp. 208–21.

Bagley, C., Mallick, K. and Verma, G. K. (1979). 'Pupil self-esteem: a study of black and white teenagers in British schools', in G. K. Verma and C. Bagley (eds), *Race, Education and Identity*, London: The Macmillan Press, pp. 176–91.

Baily, J. (1990). '*Qawwali* in Bradford: traditional music in Muslim communities', in P. Oliver (ed.), *Black Music in Britain: Essays on the Afro-Asian contribution to Popular Music*, Milton Keynes: Open University Press, pp. 153–65.

Ballard, C. (1979). 'Conflict, continuity and change: second-generation South Asians', in V. S. Khan (ed.), *Minority Families in Britain: Support and Stress*, London: Macmillan Press, pp. 109–30.

Ballard, R. (1982). 'South Asian families', in R. and R. Rapoport, *Families in Britain*, London: Routledge and Kegan Paul, pp. 179–204.

Ballard, R. (1989). 'The Sikhs in Britain', in N. G. Barrier and V. A. Dusenbery (eds), *The Sikh Diaspora: Migration and Experience Beyond Punjab*, Delhi: Chanakya Publications, pp. 200–34.

Ballard, R. (ed.) (1994a). *Desh Pardesh: The South Asian Presence in Britain*, London: Hurst and Company.

Ballard, R. (1994b). 'Differentiation and disjunction among the Sikhs', in R. Ballard (ed.), *Desh Pardesh: The South Asian Presence in Britain*, London: Hurst and Company, pp. 88–116.

Ballard, R. (2000). 'The growth and changing character of the Sikh presence in Britain', in H. Coward, J. H. Hinnells and R. B. Williams (eds), *The South Asian Religious Diaspora in Britain, Canada and the United States*, Albany: State University of New York Press, pp. 127–44.

Ballard, R. and Vellins, S. (1985). 'South Asian entrants to British universities: a comparative note', in *New Community*, 12 (2), 260–5.

Banjeri, S. and Bauman, G. (1990). 'Bhangra 1984–1988: fusion and professionalization in a genre of South Asian dance music', in P. Oliver (ed.), *Black Music in Britain: Essays on the Afro-Asian contribution to popular music*, Buckingham: Open University Press, pp. 137–52.

Banton, M. (1977). 'The adjective 'black': a discussion note', *New Community*, 5 (4), pp. 480–2.

Banton, M. (1987). 'The battle of the name', *New Community*, 14 (1/2), 170–5.

Baraitser, P. (1999). 'Family planning and sexual health: understanding the needs of South Asian women in Glasgow', *New Community*, 25 (1), 133–49.

Beetham, D. (1967). *Immigrant School Leavers and the Youth Employment Service in Birmingham*, London: Institute of Race Relations.

Bell, D. (1980). *Sociological Journeys: Essays 1960–1980*, London: Heinemann.

Berger, P. L. (1969). *The Social Reality of Religion*, London: Faber and Faber.

Berthoud, R. and Beishon, S. (1997). 'People, families and households', in T. Modood, R. Berthoud, J. Lakey, J. Nazroo, P. Smith, S. Virdee and S. Beishon, *Ethnic Minorities in Britain: Diversity and Disadvantage*, The Fourth National Survey of Ethnic Minorities, London: The Policy Studies Institute, 18–59.

Bhachu, P. K. (1985). *Parental Educational Strategies: The Case of Punjabi Sikhs in Britain*, Research Papers in Ethnic Relations No. 3, Centre for Research in Ethnic Relations, Coventry: University of Warwick.

Bhachu, P. K. (1991). 'The East African Sikh Diaspora', in S. Vertovec (ed.), *Aspects of the South Asian Diaspora*, Oxford University Papers on India, vol. 2, part 2, Delhi: Oxford University Press, pp. 57–85.

Bourdieu, P. (1985). 'the forms of capital', in J. G. Richardson (ed.), *Handbook of Theory and Research for the Sociology of Religion*, New York, Greenwood, pp. 241–58.

Brah, A. (1978). 'South Asian teenagers in Southall: their perceptions of marriage, family and ethnic identity', *New Community*, 6 (3), 197–206.

Brah, A. (1979). 'Inter-generational and inter-ethnic perceptions: a comparative study of South Asian and English adolescents and their parents in Southall, Ph.D. thesis, Department of Education, University of Bristol.

Brah, A. (1986). 'Unemployment and racism: Asian youth on the dole', in S. Allen, A. Waton, K. Purcell and S. Wood (eds), *The Experience of Unemployment*, Basingstoke: MacMillan Press Ltd, pp. 61–78.

Brah, A. (1993). '"Race" and "culture" in the gendering of labour markets: South Asian young Muslim women and the labour market', *New Community*, 19 (3), 441–58.

Brah, A. (1996). *Cartographies of Diaspora: Contesting Identities*, London and New York: Routledge.

Brah, A. and Shaw, S. (1993). *Working Choices: South Asian Young Women and the Labour Market*, Centre for Extra-Mural Studies, Birbeck College, University of London, Research Paper Series No. 91, Sheffield: Employment Department.

Brayfield, C. (1998). 'A generation born to conform', *The Times*, 24 June 1998, 19.

Brierley, P. (2000). *The Tide is Running Out: What the English Church Attendance Survey Shows*, London: Christian Research.

British Broadcasting Corporation (BBC) (1955). *Religious Broadcasts and the Public*, London: Audience Research Department, BBC.

Bromley, C. and Curtice, J. (1999). 'Is there a third way?', in R. Jowell, J. Curtice, A. Park, K. Thomson with L. Jarvis, C. Bromley and N. Stratford (eds), *British Social Attitudes: the 16th Report*, Aldershot: Ashgate, pp. 201–233.

Brook, L., Hedges, S., Jowell, R., Lewis, J., Prior, G., Sebastian, G., Taylor, B. and Witherspoon, S. (compilers) (1992). *British Social Attitudes Cumulative Sourcebook:The First Six Surveys*, Aldershot: Gower.

Brooks, A. (1983). 'Black businesses in Lambeth: obstacles to expansion', *New Community*, 10 (1/2), 42–54.

Brooks, D. and Singh, K. (not dated, c.1976). *Aspirations Versus Opportunities: Asian and White school leavers in the Midlands*, Walsall: Walsall Council for Community Relations and Leicester Community Relations Council in conjunction with the Commission for Racial Equality.

Brown, J. (1970). *The Un-Melting Pot: An English Town and its Immigrants*, London: Macmillan.

Bruce, S, (1996). *Religion in the Modern World*, Oxford: Oxford University Press.

Bryson, A. and Gomez, R. (2002). 'Marching on together? Recent trends in union membership', in A. Park, J. Curtice, K. Thomson, L. Jarvis and C. Bromley (eds), *British Social Attitudes: The 19th Report*, National Centre for Social Research, London: Sage Publications, pp. 43–74.

Buck, N. and Scott, J. (1994). 'Household and family change', in N. Buck, J. Gershuny, D. Rose and J. Scott (eds), *Changing Households: The BHPS 1990 to 1992*, Essex: ESRC Research Centre on Micro-social Change, pp. 61–82.

Burgess, S. and Rees, H. (1994). *Lifetime Jobs and Transient Jobs: Job Tenure in Britain 1975–1992*, London: Centre for Economic Policy Research.

Butterworth, E. (1969). 'Muslims in Britain', in D. Martin (ed.), *A Sociological Yearbook of Religion in Britain 2*, London, SCM, pp. 137–156.

Carey, G. (2004). 'Christianity and Islam: collision or convergence?', lecture given by the former Archbishop of Canterbury at the Gregorian University, Rome on 25 March 2004, http://www.timmesonline.co.uk/article/0,,2-1053088,00.html

Carey, S. and Shukur, A. (1985). 'A profile of the Bangladeshi community in East London', *New Community*, 12 (3), pp. 405–17.

Clinton, B. (2001). *The Struggle for the Soul of the 21st Century*, BBC Dimbleby Lecture, 14 December 2001.

Cochrane, R. and Sukhwant, B. (1990). 'The drinking habits of Sikh, Hindu and Muslim and white men in the West Midlands: a community survey', *British Journal of Addiction*, 85 (6), 759–69.

Coleman, J. C. and Hendry, L. B. (1999, 3rd edn). *The Nature of Adolescence*, London: Routledge.

Commission for Racial Equality (1978, 2nd edn). *Between Two Cultures: A Study of Relationships between generations in the Asian Community in Britain*, London: Commission for Racial Equality.

Community Relations Commission (1977). *Urban Deprivation, Racial Inequality and Social Policy*, London: HMSO.

Cox, E. (1967). *Sixth Form Religion: a study of the beliefs and of the attitudes to religion, religious instruction, and morals, of a sample of grammar school sixth form pupils, based on an investigation sponsored by the Christian Education Movement*, London: SCM Press.

Cross, C. P. (1976/7). 'Youth clubs and coloured youths', *New Community*, 5 (4), 489–94.

Currie, R., Gilbert, A. and Horsley, L. (1977). *Churches and Churchgoers: Patterns of Church Growth in the British Isles since 1700*, Oxford: Clarendon Press.

Curtis, J. and Jowell, R. (1997). 'Trust in the political system', in R. Jowell, J, Curtice, A. Park, Brook, K. Thomson and C. Bryson (eds), *British Social Attitudes: The 14th Report*, Aldershot: Ashgate, pp. 89–109.

Darsh, S. M. (1984). *An Outline of Islamic Family Law*, London: Ta Ha Publishers.

Davie, G. (1994). *Religion in Britain since 1945*, Oxford: Blackwell Publishers Ltd.

Demir, M. and Urberg, K. A. (2004). 'Church attendance and well-being among adolescents', *Journal of Beliefs and Values*, 25 (1), 63–8.

Department of Education and Employment (1996). *Youth Cohort Study: Trends in the Activities and Experiences of 16–18 year olds: England and Wales: 1985–1994*, issue 7 (96), London: The Stationery Office.

Department of Education and Employment (1997). *Youth Cohort Study: The Activities and Experiences of 16 year olds: England and Wales: 1996*, issue 8 (97), London: The Stationery Office.

Department of Education and Employment (1998). *Youth Cohort Study: The Activities and Experiences of 18 year olds: England and Wales: 1996*, issue 13 (98), London: The Stationery Office.

Department of Education and Employment (1999a). *Youth Cohort Studies: The Activities and Experiences of 16 year olds: England and Wales: 1998*, issue 4 (99), London: The Stationery Office.

Department of Education and Employment (1999b). *Youth Cohort Studies: The Activities and Experiences of 18 year olds: England and Wales: 1998*, issue 5 (99), London: The Stationery Office.

Department of Education and Science (1967). *Immigrants and the Youth Service*, Report of a Committee of the Youth Service Development Council, London: HMSO.

Dickinson, L., Hobbs, A., Kleinberg, S. M. and Martin, P. J. (1975). *The Immigrant School Learner: A Study of Pakistani Pupils in Glasgow*, Slough: NFER Publishing Company Ltd.

Dosanjh, J. S. (n.d.). *Punjabi Immigrant Children: Their Social and Educational Problems in Adjustment*, Institute of Education, Nottingham: University of Nottingham.

Drew, D. (1995). *'Race', Education and Work: The Statistics of Inequality*, Aldershot: Avebury.

Drew, D., Gray, J. and Sime, N. (1992). *Against the Odds: The Education and Labour Market Experiences of Black Young People*, Research and Development No 68, Youth Cohort Series 19, Sheffield: Department of Employment.

Drury, B. M. (1988). Ethnicity amongst second generation Sikh girls: a case study in Nottingham, Ph.D. thesis, Nottingham: University of Nottingham.

Drury, B. M. (1991). 'Sikh girls and the maintenance of an ethnic culture', *New Community*, 17 (3), 387–99.

Drury, B. M. (1996). 'The impact of religion, culture, racism and politics on the multiple identities of Sikh girls', in T. Ranger, Y. Samad and O. Stuart (eds), *Culture, Identity and Politics: Ethnic Minorities in Britain*, Aldershot: Avebury, pp.99–111.

Eade, J. (1989). *The Politics of Community: The Bangladeshi Community in East London*, Aldershot: Avebury.

Eade, J. (1992). 'Quests for belonging', in A. Cambridge and S. Feuchtwang (eds), *Where you Belong*, Aldershot: Avebury.

Eppel, E. M. and Eppel, M. (1966). *Adolescents and Morality: A Study of Some Moral Values and Dilemmas of Working Adolescents in the Context of a Changing Climate of Opinion*, London: Routledge and Kegan Paul.

Fane, R. S. (1999). 'Is self-assigned religious affiliation socially significant?', in L. J. Frances (ed.), *Sociology, Theology and the Curriculum*, London: Cassell, pp. 113–124.

Ferriman, A. (1999). 'England launches campaign on teenage pregnancies', in *The British Medical Journal*, 19 June 1999.

Field, F. and Haikin, P. (1971). *Black Britons*, London: Oxford University Press.

Field, S. (1984). *The Attitudes of Ethnic Minorities: A Home Office Research and Planning Unit Report*, London: HMSO.

Field, S., Mair, G., Rees, T. and Stevens, P. (eds) (1981). *Ethnic Minorities in Britain: A Study of Trends in their Position since 1961*, London: HMSO.

Fogelman, K. (ed.), (1976). *Britain's Sixteen-Year-Olds*, London: National Children's Bureau.

Fowler, B., Littlewood, B. and Madigan, R. (1977). 'Immigrant school leavers and the search for work', *Sociology*, 65–85.

Francis, L. J. (1982). *Youth In Transit: A Profile of 16–25 Year Olds*, Aldershot: Gower.

Francis, L. J. (1984). *Teenagers and the Church*, London: Collins.

Francis, L. J. (1996). 'The relationship between Eysenck's personality factors and attitude towards substance use among 13- to 15-year-olds', *Personality and Individual Differences*, 21 (5), 633–40.

Francis, L. J. (1997). 'Christianity, personality and concern about environmental pollution among 13- to 15-year-olds', *Journal of Beliefs and Values*, 18 (1), 7–16.

Francis, L. J. and Katz, Y. J. (2002). 'Religiosity and happiness: a study among Israeli female undergraduates', *Research in the Social Scientific Study of Religion*, 13, 75–86.

Francis, L. J. and Kay, W. K. (1995). *Teenage Religion and Values*, Leominster: Gracewing.

Francis, L. J. and Lester, D. (1997). 'Religion, personality, and happiness' *Journal of Contemporary Religion*, 12, 81–6.

Francis, L. J. and Mullen, K. (1993). 'Religiosity and attitudes towards drug use among 13–15 year olds in England', *Addiction*, 88 (5), 665–72.

Francis, L. J. and Robbins, M. (2000). 'Religion and happiness: a study in empirical theology', *Transpersonal Psychology Review*, 4, 17–22.

Furnham, A. and Gunter, B. (1989). *The Anatomy of Adolescence: Young People's Social Attitudes in Britain*, London: Routledge.

Gardner, J. and Oswald, A. (2001). 'Internet use: the digital divide', in A. Park, J. Curtice, K. Thomson, L. Jarvis and C. Bromley (eds), *British Social Attitudes Survey: The 18th Report*, Sage: London, pp. 159–73.

Gaskin, K., Vlaeminke, M. and Fenton, N. (1996). *Young People's Attitudes to the Voluntary Sector*, London, The Commission on the Future of the Voluntary Sector.

Geddes, A. (1993). 'Asian and Afro-Caribbean representation in elected local government in England and Wales', *New Community*, 20 (1), 43–58.

Gershuny, J. and Brice, J. (1994). 'Looking backwards: family and work 1900 to 1992', in N. Buck, J. Gershuny, D. Rose and J. Scott (eds), *Changing Households: The BHPS 1990 to 1992*, Essex: ESRC Research Centre on Micro-social Change, pp. 27–60.

Get Connected (2002). *Still No Idea*, reported in *The Times*, 30 December 2002: 7.

Ghuman, P. A. S. (1980). 'Bhattra Sikhs in Cardiff: family and kinship organization', *New Community*, 8 (3), 308–16.

Ghuman, P. A. S. (1994). *Coping with Two Cultures: British Asian and Indo-Canadian Adolescents*, Clevedon: Multilingual Matters Ltd.

Ghuman, P. A. S. (1999). *Asian Adolescents in the West*, Leicester: British Psychological Society Books.

Gill, R. (1993). *The Myth of the Empty Church*, London: SPCK.

Gill, R. (1999). *Churchgoing and Christian Ethics*, Cambridge: Cambridge University Press.

Gill, R. (2003). *The 'Empty' Church Revisited*, Aldershot: Ashgate.

Gorer, G. (1955). *Exploring English Character*, London: Cresset Press.

Gorsuch, R. L. (1995). 'Religious aspects of substance abuse and recovery', *Journal of Social Issues*, 51, 65–83.

Gould, A., Shaw, A. and Ahrendt, D. (1996). 'Illegal drugs: liberal and restrictive attitudes', in R. Jowell, J. Curtice, A. Park, L. Brook and K. Thomson (eds), *British Social Attitudes: The 13th Report*, Social and

Community Planning Research, Aldershot: Dartmouth Publishing Company, pp. 93–116.

Graff, N. D. de and Need, A. (2000). 'Losing faith: is Britain alone?', in R. Jowell, J. Curtice, A. Park, K. Thomson, L. Jarvis, C. Bromley and N. Stratford (eds), *British Social Attitudes: The 17th Report*', London: Sage Publications, pp. 119–36.

Greeley, A. M. (1972). *Unsecular Man: The Persistence of Religion*, New York: Shocken Books.

Gupta, Y. P. (1977). 'The educational and vocational aspirations of Asian immigrant and English school-leavers: a comparative study', *The British Journal of Sociology*, 28 (2), 185–98.

Hall, P. A. (1999). 'Social capital in Britain', *The British Journal of Political Science*, 29 (3), 417–61.

Halpern, D. (1995). 'Values, morals and modernity: the values, constrains and norms of European youth', in M. Rutter and D. J. Smith (eds), *Psychosocial Disorders in Young People: Time Trends and their Causes*, Chichester: John Wiley and Sons, pp. 324–87.

Halstead, J. M. (1986). *The Case for Muslim Voluntary-Aided Schools*, Cambridge: The Islamic Academy.

Halstead, M. (1988). *Education, Justice and Cultural Diversity: An Examination of the Honeyford Sffair, 1984–1985*, London: Falmer Press.

Hammond, P. (1985). *The Sacred in a Secular Age*, Berkeley: University of California Press.

Hargreaves, D. J. (1967). *Social Relations in a Secondary School*, London: Routledge and Kegan Paul.

Harris Research Centre (1993). *Black and Asian Attitudes to the Arts in Birmingham*, a report prepared for the Arts Council of Great Britain, Richmond: Harris Research Centre.

Hashnie, F. (1967). *The Pakistani Family in Britain*, London: National Committee for Commonwealth Immigrants.

Hasnie, N. (1977). *The Way Ahead: A survey of Asian Youth in Huddersfield*, Huddersfield: Kirklees Metropolitan Council.

Heald, G. and Wybrow, R. J. (1986). *The Gallup Survey of Britain*, London: Croom Helm.

Helweg, A. W. (1979). *Sikhs in England*, Delhi: Oxford University Press.

Henderson, M. (1998). 'Generation Y: young, gifted and self-centred', *The Times*, 14 November 1998, 20.

Hendry, L. B., Shucksmith, J., Love, J. G. and Glendinning, A. (1993). *Young People's Leisure and Lifestyles*, London: Routledge.

Henley, A. (1983a). *Caring for Hindus and their Families: Religious Aspects of Care*, London: HHC/DHSS/King Edward's Hospital Fund for London.

Henley, A. (1983b). *Caring for Sikhs and their Families: Religious Aspects of Care*, London: HHC/DHSS/ King Edward's Hospital Fund for London.

Henley, A. (1983c). *Caring for Muslims and their Families: religious aspect of care*, London: HHC/DHSS/King Edward's Hospital Fund for London.

Hewitt, I. B. (1993). *What does Islam say about . . . ? Islam and major issues for GCSE coursework*, London: The Muslim Educational Trust.

Hilton, J. (1972). 'The ambitions of school children', *Race Today*, March, 79–81.

Hiro, D. (1972, revised). *The Indian Family in Britain*, London: Community Relations Commission.

Hiro, D. (1991). *Black British, White British*, London: Grafton.

Hiskett, M. (1989). *Schooling for British Muslims: Integrated, Opted-out or Denominational?* London: The Social Affairs Unit, Research Report 12.

Home Office (2004). *Draft Report on Young Muslims and Extremism*, http://www.globalsecurity.org/security/library/report/2004/muslimext-uk.htm

Huntington, S. P. (1996). *The Clash of Civilisations and the Remaking of World Order*, New York: Simon and Schuster.

Husband, C. (1994). 'The political context of Muslim communities' participation in British society', in B. Lewis and D. Schnapper (eds), *Muslims in Europe*, London: Pinter.

Hutnik, N. (1991). *Ethnic Minority Identity: A Social Psychological Perspective*, Oxford: Clarendon Press.

Inglehart, R. (1990). *Culture Shift in Advanced Industrial Society*, Princetown: Princetown University Press.

Institute for the Study of Islam and Christianity (2005). *Islam in Britain: the British Muslim Community in February 2005*, Pewsey: Isaac Publishing.

Iqbal, M. (1975). *Islamic Education and Single Sex Schools*, London: Union of Muslim Organizations of UK and Eire.

Jackson, R. and Killingley, D. (1991). *Moral Issues in the Hindu Tradition*, Stoke-on-Trent: Trentham Books.

James, A. G. (1974). *Sikh Children in Britain*, Institute of Race Relations, London: Oxford University Press.

Jeffery, P. (1976). *Migrants and Refugees: Muslim and Christian Families in Bristol*, Cambridge: Cambridge University Press.

John, D. (1969). *Indian Workers' Associations in Britain*, London: Oxford University Press.

Johnston, M. and Jowell, R. (2001). 'How robust is British civil society?', in A. Park, J. Curtice, K. Thomson, L. Jarvis and C. Bromley (eds), *British Social Attitudes: The 18th Report*, London: Sage, pp. 175–97.

Joly, D. (1987). 'Association amongst the Pakistani population in Britain', in J. Rex, D. Joly and C. Wilpert (eds), *Immigrant Associations in Europe*, Aldershot: Gower, pp. 62–85.

Joly, D. (1988). 'Making a place for Islam in British schools', in T. Gerholm and Y. G. Lithman (eds), *The New Islamic Presence in Western Europe*, London: Mansell, pp. 32–52.

Bibliography

Joly, D. (1995). *Britannia's Crescent: Making a Place for Muslims in British Society*, Aldershot: Avebury.

Jones, T. (1981/2). 'Small business developments and the Asian community in Britain', *New Community*, 9 (3), 467–77.

Jones, T. (1993). *Britain's Ethnic Minorities*, London: Policy Studies Institute.

Kalra, S. S. (1980). *Daughters of Tradition: Adolescent Sikh Girls and their Accommodation to life in British Society*, Birmingham: Third World Publications.

Kanitkar, H. (1979). 'A school for Hindus?', *New Community*, 7 (2), 178–83.

Kannan, C. T. (1978). *Cultural Adaptation of Asian Immigrants: First and Second Generation*, published by the author.

Kay, W. K. and Francis, L. J. (1996). *Drift from the Churches: Attitude Toward Christianity during Childhood and Adolescence*, Cardiff: University of Wales Press.

Khera, A. K. (1981). 'The status of women in Hindu society', in D. G. Bowen (ed.), *Hinduism in England*, The Faculty of Contemporary Studies, Bradford: Bradford College, pp. 98–109.

King, J. (1994). *Three Asian Associations*, Monographs in Ethnic Relations No. 8, Centre for Research in Ethnic Relations, Coventry: University of Warwick.

Kohli, S. S. (1974). *Sikh Ethics*, Delhi: Munshiram Manoharlal Publishers Pvt. Ltd.

Knott, K. (1986). *Hinduism in Leeds: A Study of Religious Practice in the Indian Hindu Community and in Hindu-related Groups*, Community Religions Project Monograph, Leeds: Department of Theology and Religious Studies, University of Leeds.

Knott, K. (1992). *The Changing Character of the Religions of the Ethnic Minorities of Asian Origin in Britain: Final Report of a Leverhulme Project*, Community Religions Project, Research Papers (New Series), no. 11, Leeds: Department of Theology and Religious Studies, University of Leeds.

Knott, K. (1994). 'The Gujarati Mochis in Leeds: from leather stockings to surgical boots and beyond', in R. Ballard (ed.), *Desh Pardesh: the South Asian Presence in Britain*, London: Hurst and Company, pp. 213–30.

Knott, K. and Khokher, S. (1993). 'Religious and ethnic identity among young Muslim women in Bradford', *New Community*, 19 (4), 593–610.

Leach, G. (1999). *The End of Altruism?*, London: Institute of Directors.

Lechner, F. J. (1991). 'The case against secularization: a rebuttal', *Social Forces*, 69, 1103–19.

Lechner, F. J. (1996). 'Rejoinder to Stark and Iannaccone: 'Heads I win . . .': on immunizing a theory', *Journal for the Scientific Study of Religion*, 35, 272–74.

Le Lohé, M. J. (1989). 'The performance of Asian and Black candidates in the British general election of 1987', *New Community*, 15 (2), 159–70.
Lewis, P. (1994b). *Islamic Britain: Religion, Politics and Identity among British Muslims*, London: I. B. Tauris.
Lewis, P. (1996). *The Function, Education and Influence of the 'Ulama in Bradford's Muslim Community*, Community Research Project, Research Project (New Paper), Leeds: University of Leeds.
Livingstone, P. (1977). *The Leisure Needs of Asian Boys aged 8–14 in Slough, Berkshire*, London: The Scout Association.
Louden, D. M. (1978a). 'Self-esteem and locus of control: some findings on immigrant adolescents in Britain', *New Community*, 6 (3), 218–34.
Louden, D. M. (1978b). 'Self-esteem and locus of control in minority group adolescents', *Ethnic and Racial Studies*, 1 (2), 196–217.
Louden, D. M. (1980). 'A comparative study of self-esteem among minority group adolescents in Britain', *Journal of Adolescents*, 3 (1), 17–33.
Lyon, M. H. and West, B. M. J. (1995). 'London Patels: caste and commerce', *New Community*, 21 (3), 399–419.
McGlone, F., Park, A. and Roberts, C. (1996). 'Relative values: kinship and friendship', in R. Jowell, J. Curtice, A. Park, L. Brook and K. Thomson (eds), *British Social Attitudes: The 13th Report*, Social and Community Planning Research, Aldershot: Dartmouth Publishing Company, 53–72.
McGrath, M. (1976). 'The economic position of immigrants in Batley', *New Community*, 5 (3), 239–49.
McLaren, L. and Johnson, M. (2004). 'Understanding the rising tide of anti-immigrant sentiment', in A. Park, J. Curtice, K. Thompson, C. Bromley and M. Phillips (eds), *British Social Attitudes: The 21st Report*, London: Sage, pp. 169–200.
McLean, M. (1985). 'Private supplementary schools and the ethnic challenge to state education in Britain', in C. Brock and W. Tulasiewicz (eds), *Cultural Identity and Educational Policy*, London: Croom Helm, pp. 326–45.
McLeod, W. H. (1989). *Who is a Sikh? The Problem of Sikh Identity*, Oxford: Clarendon Press.
Martin, D. (1969). *The Religious and the Secular: Studies in Secularization*, London: Routledge and Kegan Paul.
Martin, D. (1978). *A General Theory of Secularization*, London: Blackwell Publishers Ltd.
Mason, D. (1990). 'A Rose by any other Name . . .? categorisation, identity and social science', *New Community* 17 (1), 123–33.
Mass-Observation (1947). *Puzzled People: A Study in Popular Attitudes to Religion, Ethics, Progress and Politics in a London Borough*, London: Gollancz.
Matthews, D. A., McCullough, M. E., Larson, D. B., Koenig, H. G., Swyers, J. P. and Milano, M. G. (1998). 'Religious commitment and

health status: a review of the research and implications for family medicine', *Archives of Family Medicine*, 7, 118–24.

Mizra, K. (1989). *The Silent Cry: Second Generation Bradford Muslim Women Speak*, Research Paper No. 43, Birmingham: Centre for the Study of Islam and Christian-Muslim Relations.

Modood, T. (1988). '"Black", racial equality and Asian identity', *New Community*, 14 (3), 397–404.

Modood, T. (1997). 'Culture and identity', in T. Modood, R. Berthoud, J. Lakey, J. Nazroo, P. Smith, S. Virdee and S. Beishon, *Ethnic Minorities in Britain: Diversity and Disadvantage*, The Fourth National Survey of Ethnic Minorities, London: The Policy Studies Institute, pp. 290–338.

Modood, T., Beishon, S. and Virdee, S. (1994). *Changing Ethnic Identities*, London: Policy Studies Institute.

Murad, K. (1986). *Muslim Youth in the West: Towards a New Education Strategy*, London: The Islamic Foundation.

Murray, C. and Dawson, A. (1983). *Five Thousand Adolescents: Their Attitudes, Characteristics and Attainments*, Manchester: Centre for Youth Studies, Faculty of Education, University of Manchester.

Nagra, J. S. (1981/2). 'Asian supplementary schools: a case study in Coventry', *New Community*, 9 (3), 431–6.

National Association of Young Muslims Newsletters, Leicester, 1 (1984) – 11 (1987).

Nazroo, J. Y. (1997). *The Health of Britain's Ethnic Minorities: Findings from a National Survey*. London: Policy Studies Institute.

Nesbitt, E. M. (1990a). 'Pitfalls in religious taxonomy: Hindus and Sikhs, Valmikis and Ravidasis', *Religion Today*, 6 (1), 9–12.

Nesbitt, E. M. (1990b). 'Religion and identity: the Valmiki community in Coventry', *New Community*, 16 (2), 261–74.

Nesbitt, E. M. (1991). *'My Dad's Hindu, My Mum's side are Sikhs': issues in Religious Identity*, Arts, Culture, Education, Research and Curriculum Paper, Charlbury: National Foundation for Arts Education.

Nesbitt, E. M. (1994). 'Valmikis in Coventry', in R. Ballard (ed.), *Desh Pardesh: The South Asian Presence in Britain*, London: Hurst and Company, pp. 117–41.

Nesbitt, E. M. (1995). 'The religious lives of Sikh children in Coventry', unpublished Ph.D. thesis, Coventry: University of Warwick.

Nesbitt, E. M. and Jackson, R. (1993–4). 'Aspects of cultural transmission in a diaspora Sikh community', *Journal of Sikh Studies*, 18, 49–67, Amritsar: Guru Nanak Dev University.

Nesbitt, E. M. and Jackson, R. (1995). 'Sikh children's use of 'God': ethnographic fieldwork and religious education', *British Journal of Religious Education*, 17 (2), 108–20.

Newbigin, L. (1989). *The Gospel in a Pluralist Society*, London: SPCK.

Nielsen, J. S. (2000). 'Muslims in Britain: ethnic minorities, community or ummah?', in H. Coward, J. H. Hinnells and R. B. Williams (eds), *The South Asian Religious Diaspora in Britain, Canada and the United States*, Albany: State University of New York Press, pp. 109–125.

Noller, P. and Callan, V. (1991). *The Adolescent in the Family*, London: Routledge.

Omran, A. R. (1992). *Family Planning in the Legacy of Islam*, London: Routledge.

Owen, D. (1996). *Towards 2001: Ethnic Minorities and the Census*, Warwick: Centre for Research in Ethnic Relations, University of Warwick.

Park, A. (1995). 'Teenagers and their politics', in R. Jowell, J. Curtice, A. Park, L. Brook and D. Ahrendt with K. Thomson (eds), *British Social Attitudes: The 12th Report*, Socialand Community Planning Research, Aldershot: Dartmouth Publishing Company, pp. 43–60.

Park, A. (1999). 'Young people and political apathy', in R. Jowell, J. Curtice, A. Park, K. Thomson with L. Jarvis, C. Bromley and N. Stratford (eds), *British Social Attitudes; the 16th report*, Aldershot: Ashgate, 23–44.

Park, A. (2000). 'The generation game', in R. Jowell, J. Curtice, A. Park, K. Thomson, L. Javis, C. Bromley and N. Stratford (eds), *British Social Attitudes: The 17th Report*, Aldershot: Ashgate, pp. 1–22.

Park, A. (2004). 'Has modern politics disenchanted the young?', in A. Park, J. Curtice, K. Thompson, C. Bromley and M. Phillips (eds), *British Social Attitudes: The 21st Report*, London: Sage, pp. 23–47.

Peach, C. (2005). 'Muslims in the UK', in T. Abbas (ed.), *Muslim Britain: Communities under Pressure*, London: Zed Books, pp. 8–30.

Penn, R. and Scattergood, H. (1992). 'Ethnicity and career aspirations in contemporary Britain', *New Community*, 19 (1), 75–98.

Pharoah, C. and Tanner, S. (1997). 'Trends in charitable giving', in *Fiscal Studies*, 18 (4), pp. 427–43.

Phillips, M. (2004). 'Teenagers on family values', in A. Park, J. Curtice, K. Thompson, C. Bromley and M. Phillips (eds), *British Social Attitudes: The 21st Report*, London: Sage, 49–71.

Putnam, R. D. (1993). *Making Democracy Work*, Princeton, Princeton University Press.

Putnam, R. D. (1996). 'The strange disappearance of civil America', *The American Prospect* (Winter), 34–49.

Putnam, R. D. (2000). *Bowling Alone: The Collapse and Revival of American Community*, New York, Simon and Schuster.

Rae, D. (2002). Foreword, in S. L. McLean, D. A. Schultz and M. B. Steger, *Social Capital: Critical Perspectives on Community and 'Bowling Alone'*, New York, New York University Press.

Ranger, T., Samad, Y. and Stuart, O. (eds), (1996). *Culture, Identity and Politics: Ethnic Minorities in Britain*, Aldershot: Avebury.

Raza, M. S. (1993, 2nd edn). *Islam in Britain: Past, Present and Future*, Leicester: Volcano Press.

Rex, J. and Tomlinson, S. (1979). *Colonial Immigrants in a British City: A Class Analysis*, London: Routledge and Kegan Paul.

Richardson, R. (ed.), with Muir, H. and Smith, L. (2004). *Islamophobia: issues, Challenges and Action*. Report by the Commission on British Muslims and Islamophobia, Stoke-on-Trent: Uniting Britain Trust.

Roberts, H. and Sachdev, D. (eds), (1996). *Young People's Social Attitudes: Having their Ssay – The Views of 12–19 year olds*, Ilford: Barnardos.

Robinson, V. and Flintoff, I. (1982). 'Asian retailing in Coventry', *New Community*, 10 (2), 251–8.

Roy, A. (2001). 'Indians try to escape catch-all "Asian" tag', *Telegraph*, 19 June.

Runnymede Trust (1974/5). 'Trade unions and immigrant workers', *New Community*, 4 (1), 19–36.

Russell, H. (1998). 'The rewards of work', in R. Jowell, J. Curtice, A. Park, L. Brook, K. Thomson and D. Bryson (eds), *British – and European – Social Attitudes: The 15th Report*, Aldershot: Ashgate, pp. 77–97.

Rutter, M. and Smith, D. J. (eds), (1995). *Psychosocial Disorders in Young People: Time Trends and their Causes*, Chichester: John Wiley and Sons.

Saeed, S. and Galbraith, J. I. (1981/2). 'Attitudes of Asian children to the police', *New Community*, 9 (3), 447–53.

Saifullah-Khan, V. (1974). 'Pakistani villagers in a British City', Ph.D. thesis, Bradford: University of Bradford.

Sarwar, G. (1982, 2nd edn). *Islam: Beliefs and Teachings*, London: The Muslim Educational Trust.

Sarwar, G. (1989). *What can Muslims do?*, London: The Muslim Educational Trust.

Sarwar, G. (1992, 2nd edn). *Sex Education: The Muslim Perspective*, London: The Muslim Educational Trust.

Sarwar, G. (1994, revised edn). *British Muslims and Schools*, London: The Muslim Educational Trust.

Schofield, M. (1965). *The Sexual Behaviour of Young People*, London: Longmans.

Scott, A., Pearce, D. and Goldblatt, P. (2001). *The Size and Characteristics of the Minorit Ethnic Populations of Great Britain – latest estimates: regional distribution in 2000*, The Office for National Statistics, http://www.statistics.gov.uk/CCI/article.asp?ID=580&Pos=3&ColRank=1&Rank=176

Scott, J., Braun, M. and Alwin, D. (1998). 'Partner, parent, worker: family and gender roles', in R. Jowell, J. Curtice, A. Park, L. Brook, K. Thomson and D. Bryson (eds), *British – and European – Social Attitudes: The 15th Report*, Aldershot: Ashgate, pp. 19–37.

Seyd, P., Whiteley, P. and Parry, J. (1996). *Labour and Conservative Party Members 1990–1992: Social Characteristics, Political Attitudes and Activities*, Aldershot: Dartmouth.

Shaikh, S. and Kelly A. (1989). 'To mix or not to mix? Pakistani girls in British schools', *Educational Research*, 31(1) 10–19.

Sharma, S. M. (1980). 'Perceptions of political institutions among Asians and English adolescents in Britain', *New Community*, 8 (3), 240–7.

Shaw, A. (1988). *A Pakistani Community in Britain*, Oxford: Blackwell.

Siddiqui, K. (1990). *The Muslim Manifesto: A Strategy for Survival*, London: The Muslim Institute.

Sigelman, L. (1977). 'Review of the polls: multi-national surveys of religious beliefs', *Journal for the Scientific Study of Religion*, 16 (3), 289–94.

Silbereisen, R. K., Robins, L. and Rutter, M. (1995). 'Secular trends in substance use: concepts and data on the impact of social change on alcohol and drug abuse', in M. Rutter and D. J. and Smith (eds), *Psychosocial Disorders in Young People: Time Trends and their Causes*, Chichester: John Wiley and Sons, pp. 490–543.

Sills, A., Tarpey, M. and Golding, P. (1983). 'Asians in an inner city', *New Community*, 10 (1/2), 34–41.

Simmons, C. and Wade, W. (1984). *I'd Like to Say What I Think: A Study of Attitudes, Values and Beliefs of Young People Today*, London: Kogan Page.

Simons, J. (1982). 'Attitude to family size among immigrant Sikhs in London', in D. A. Coleman (ed.), *Demography of Immigrants and Minority Groups in the United Kingdom*, London: Academic Press, pp. 169–92.

Singh, R. (1992). *Immigrants to Citizens: The Sikh Community in Bradford*, The Race Relations Research Unit, Bradford: Department of Contemporary Studies, Bradford and Ilkley Community College.

Smith, A. G. C. (2002). 'The nature and significance of religion among adolescents in the Metropolitan Borough of Walsall, thesis submitted for the degree of Doctor of Philosophy, University of Wales (Bangor).

Smith, A. G. C. (2005). 'Listening to the People', in J. Martineau, L. J. Francis and P. Francis (eds), *Changing Rural Life*, Norwich, Canterbury Press, pp. 193–213.

Stack, S (1991). 'The effect of religiosity on suicide in Sweden: a time series analysis', *Journal for the Scientific Study of Religion*, 30 (4), 462–8.

Stark, R. and Bainbridge, W. S. (1987). *A Theory of Religion*, New Brunswick: Rutgers University Press.

Stark, R. and Iannaccone, L. R. (1994). 'A supply-side reinterpretation of the 'secularization' of Europe', *Journal for the Scientific Study of Religion*, 33 (3), 230–52.

Still No Idea (2002). Report produced by the organization Get Connected.

Stopes-Roe, M. and Cochrane, R. (1990). *Citizens of this Country: The Asian-British*, Clevedon: Multilingual Matters Ltd.
Studlar, D. T. (1983). 'The ethnic vote, 1983: problems of analysis and interpretation', *New Community*, 11 (1/2), 92–100.
Swann, M. (1985). *Education for All: the report of the committee of inquiry into the education of children from ethnic minority groups*, London: HMSO.
Tarling, R. and Dowds, L. (1997). 'Crime and punishment', in R. Jowell, J, Curtice, A. Park, L. Brook, K. Thomson and C. Bryson (eds), *British Social Attitudes: The 14th Report*, Aldershot: Ashgate, pp. 197–214.
Tatla, D. S. (1993a). 'The Punjab crisis and Sikh mobilisation in Britain', in R. Barot (ed), *Religion and Ethnicity: Minorities and Social Change in the Metropolis*, Kampen: Kok Publishing House, pp. 96–109.
Tatla, D. S. (1993b). 'The Oolitics of Homeland: a study of ethnic linkages and political mobilisation amongst Sikhs in Britain and North America', Ph.D. thesis, Warwick: Centre for Research in Ethnic Relations, University of Warwick.
Tatla, D. S. (1999). *The Sikh Diaspora: The Search for Statehood*, London: University College London Press.
Taylor, I., Evans, K. and Fraser, P. (1996). *A Tale of Two Cities: Global Change, Local Feeling and Everyday Life and the North of England: a study of Manchester and Sheffield*, London and New York: Routledge.
Taylor, J. H. (1973a). 'High unemployment and coloured school leavers: the Tyneside pattern', *New Community*, 2 (1), 85–89.
Taylor, J. H. (1973b). 'Newcastle-on-Tyne: Asian pupils do better than whites', *British Journal of Sociology*, 24 (4), 431–48.
Thompson, M. (1974). 'The second generation: Punjabi or English?' *New Community*, 3 (3), 242–8.
Timms, N. (1992). *Family and Citizenship: Values in Contemporary Britain*, Aldershot: Dartmouth Publishing Company.
Tinker, H. (1977). *The Banyan Tree: Overseas Emigrants from Indian, Pakistan, and Bangladesh*, Oxford: Oxford University Press.
Tschannen, O. (1991). 'The secularization paradigm: a systematization', *Journal for the Scientific Study of Religion*, 30, 395–415.
Tyler, M. (1978). *Advisory and Counselling Services for Young People*, London: HMSO.
Verma, G. K. and Ashworth, B. (1986). *Ethnicity and Educational Achievement in British Schools*, London: Macmillan.
Verma, G. K. and Bagley, C. (1975). *Race and Education across Cultures*, London: Heinemann.
Verma, G. K. and Darby, D. S. (1994). *Winners and Losers: Ethnic Minorities in Sport and Recreation*, London: Falmer Press.
Verma, G. K. and Mallick, K. (1988). 'Self-esteem and educational achievement in British young South Asians', in G. K. Verma and

P. Pumfrey (eds), *Educational Attainments: Issues and Outcomes in Multicultural Education*, London: The Falmer Press.
Vertovec, S. (1996). 'On the reproduction and representation of Hinduism in Britain', in T. Ranger, Y. Samad and O. Stuart (eds), *Culture, Identity and Politics: Ethnic Minorities in Britain*, Aldershot: Avebury, pp. 77–89.
Verweij, J., Ester, P. and Nauta, R. (1997). 'Secularization as an economic and cultural phenomenon: a cross-national analysis', *Journal for the Scientific Study of Religion*, 36, 309–24.
Visram, R. (2002). *Asians in Britain: 400 Years of History*, London: Pluto.
Wahhab, I. (1989). *Muslims in Britain: Profile of a Community*, London: Runnymede Trust.
Warrier, S. (1994). 'Gujarati Prajapatis in London: family roles and sociability networks', in R. Ballard (ed.), *Desh Pardesh: the South Asian Presence in Britain*, London: Hurst and Company, pp. 191–212.
Weber, M. (1965, 4th edn, English version). *The Sociology of Religion*, London: Methuen and Co Ltd.
Wellings, K., Field, J., Johnson, A. M. and Wadsworth, J. (eds) with Bradshaw, S. (1994). *Sexual Behaviour in Britain: The National Survey of Sexual Attitudes and Lifestyle*, London: Penguin Books.
Werbner, P. (1990). *The Migration Process: Capital, Gifts and Offerings Among British Pakistanis*, Oxford: Berg.
White, R. M. (1979). 'What's in a name? Problems in official and legal uses of 'race'', *New Community*, 7 (3), 333–49.
Wilkinson, H. and Mulgan, G. (1995). *Freedom's Children: work, relationships and Politics for the 18–34 Year Olds in Britain Today*, London, Demos.
Wilkinson, I. (1988). *Muslim Beliefs and Practices in a Non-Muslim Country: A Study of Rochdale*, Research Papers: Muslims in Europe, No. 39, Birmingham: Centre for the Study of Islam and Christian-Muslim Relations.
Willmott, P. (1966). *Adolescent Boys of East London*, London: Routledge and Kegan Paul.
Wilson, A. (1978). *Finding a Voice: Asian Women in Britain*, London: Virago.
Wilson, B. (1966). *Religion in the Secular Society: A Sociological Comment*, London: Watts.
Wilson, B. (1976). *Contemporary Transformations of Religion*, London: Oxford University Press.
Wolf, R. M. (1997). 'Questionnaires', in J. P. Keeves (ed.) (2nd edn). *Educational Research, Methodology, and Measurement: an International Handbook*, Cambridge: Pergamon Press, pp. 422–27.
Woodroffe, C., Glickman, M., Barker, M. and Power, C. (1993) *Children, Teenagers and Health: The Key Data*, Buckingham: The Open University Press.

Glossary and abbreviations

Glossary

Akhirah	The Muslim belief in the afterlife
al-Muhajiroun	Radical Islamic group
Barelvi	A Muslim sect which originated in India, with an emphasis on shrines, tombs and saints
Bhatra/Bhattra/Bhattri	A Sikh subcaste, traditionally of beggars
Burqa	A face covering or veil worn by women
Divali/diwali	Hindu festival of lights
Gurdwara	A Sikh temple or meeting place
Gurpurb	The anniversaries in the life of the Guru
Haram	That which is forbidden by Islamic law
Hijab	A veil worn by Muslim women
Izzat	Family honour
Jat	A caste of Sikh peasant landowners in the Punjab
Jati	An endogamous group, usually with a common occupation
Jilbab	Dress worn by Muslim women, which leaves only the hands and face exposed
Kirpan	A dagger carried by Sikhs
Mandir	Hindu temple
Madrasa	Quranic school or college, usually associated with a mosque
Patel	A caste, originally associated with agriculture

Prajapatis	A Gujurati caste, originally made up of carpenters
Purdah	A curtain or veil used to screen women from men
Ravidasi	Followers of Ravidas, a religious group with its origins in Sikhism
Shalwar-kamiz	Baggy cotton trousers and knee-length top
Shi'ite	A member of the *Shi'a* branch of Islam
Sunni	One who adheres to the *sunna* or customary practice of the Prophet Muhammad. The word is used as the name for the largest branch of Islam
Umma(h)	Community, people, nation
Valmiki	A *zat* from the Punjab
Zakat	The Muslim giving of alms; one of the five pillars of Islam
Zat	An endogamous caste

Abbreviations

Chr	Christian
N	Number
NA	Non-affiliates, that is those adolescents who were not involved in or did not participate in any religion
n.d.	Not dated
NS	Not significant. This refers to statistical significance and is explained in the final section of Appendix 1
PSI	The Policy Studies' Institute

Index

abortion 42–53
addiction to drugs 62
advice 31–40
alcohol, underage drinking of 54–61
alcohol education 126–7
A-levels 78
al-Muhajiroun 11–12
Al Qaida 11
anorexia 23
arranged marriages 13
assimilation 120
attitudes, the effect of religion on 15–16

Begum, Shabina 10
Begum, Tasleem 13
beliefs, religious 111–18
Betts, Leah 62
Big Brother 102
Britishness 7
bulimia 23
bullying 78–84

cannabis 62–9
Carey, George 12
Children in Need 95
Christianity:
    family and friends 37
    global and national concerns 99
    leisure 74–5
    politics 107

    relationships and sexual morality 4
    religious belief 117
    right and wrong 58–9
    school 82
    substance use and abuse 6
    well-being 28–9
    work 91
church attendance 14
cigarettes 63–9
clergy 31–40
cohabitation 42
Conservative Party 103–10
contraception 43–51
council, local 103–10
crime 54–61

depression 23–30
divorce 41–53
doctors 31–40
Dosanjh, Kalvinder 13
drugs 31, 62–9, 126–7
drunkenness 63–9, 126–7

ecstasy 62
education 78–84
educationalists, implications of research for 127
Ellis, Charlene 54
employers, implications of research for 127–8
employment 85–94

environment 95–101
ethnic identity 16
European Union 8–9
exams 78–84

friends 31–40, 70–7
funerals, attendance at 21

GCSEs 78
general election 102
glue sniffing 63–9, 127
graffiti 54–61
Guantanamo Bay 10

health 123–7
heroin 63–9
Hinduism: family and friends 37–8
  global and national concerns 99
  leisure 75–6
  politics 107
  relationships and sexual morality 48–9
  religious belief 117
  right and wrong 59–60
  school 83
  substance use and abuse 67
  well-being 29
  work 91
homosexuality 42–53
honour killings 13
Hughes, Beverley 8
human rights 6

immigration 8–9, 103–10
Institute for the Study of Islam and Christianity 12
integration 9–10, 120
Internet 70
Iraq War 95
Islam: family and friends 38–9
  global and national concerns 100

leisure 76
  politics 108–9
  relationships and sexual morality 49–51
  religious belief 117
  right and wrong 60
  school 83
  substance use and abuse 67–8
  well-being 29–30
  work 92–4
Islam in Britain 120–2
Islamic dress 10
Islamophobia 10–12

jealousy 25–30

Labour Party 102–10
Lawrence, Stephen 54
leisure time 70–7
Live Aid 95
loneliness 23–30

marriage 41–53
mental health 23–30
Migration Watch UK 9, 12
multiculturalism 7, 8
Muslim community, growth of 12
Muslim Council of Great Britain 12

National Lottery 96–101
Naz, Rukhsama 13
New Age 14
non-affiliates:
  family and friends 36–7
  global and national concerns 98
  leisure 74
  politics 107
  relationships and sexual morality 47–8
  religious belief 115–16
  right and wrong 58
  school 82

substance use and abuse 66
well-being 27–8
work 90
nuclear war 95–101

parents 31–40, 70–7
police 54
politics 5–6, 102–10, 129–30
pollution 95–101
pornography 95–101
poverty, third world 95–101
Powell, Enoch 8
prayer 21
private medicine 103–10
private schools 103–10
privatization 103–10
public policy 128

racial integration 9–10
racial unrest 9
Reid, John 41
religious affiliation 18–20
religious beliefs 111–18
religious identity 16, 20
research methodology 131–2
Rushdie, Salman 11, 119

sample 133–5
Sangatte 8
SATs 78
school 78–84, 127
schools in Walsall involved in the research 134–4
secularization 13–16
self-worth, feelings of 23–30
sex education 125–6
sexual intercourse 41–53
sexual morality 41–53
sexually transmitted diseases 41
Shakespeare, Letisha 54
shoplifting 54–61
Sikhism: family and friends 39
  global and national concerns 100

leisure 76–7
politics 108–9
relationships and sexual morality 51–2
religious belief 118
right and wrong 60
school 84
substance use and abuse 68
well-being 30
work 93–4
smoking 54–61
social capital 5–7
social change 4
social policy 119–30
social security 86–95
social workers 31–40
South Asian British: family and friends 34–6
  global and national concerns 97–8
  leisure 73–4
  politics 105–6
  relationships and sexual morality 45–6
  religious belief 114–5
  right and wrong 56–8
  substance use and abuse 65–6
  school 80–1
  well-being 25–7
  work 87–90
spirituality 21
state ownership of industry 103–10
statistics, use of in the research 135
suicide 23–30

Taylor, Damilola 54
teachers and teaching 31–40, 78–84
teenage pregnancies 41
terrorism 1, 7, 11, 119
Thatcherism 6
Third World 95–101

trade unions 103–10
truancy 54–61

unemployment 85–94
United Kingdom Independence Party 8
urban unrest 9
violence, on television 95–101

Walker, Anthony 54
Walsh, Katie 62
war 95–101
weddings, attendance at 21
well-being 23–30
white British: family and friends 34–6
  global and national concerns 97–8
  leisure 73–4
  politics 105–6
  relationships and sexual morality 45–6
  religious belief 114–15
  right and wrong 56–8
  school 80–1
  substance use and abuse 65–6
  well-being 25–27
  work 87–90
work 85–94
worship, attendance at public 20–1

Yones, Heshu 13
youth centre/club 70–7
youth leader 31–40